TEXTS   PHOTOGRAPHS

Foreword

Kate Newton and Christine Rolph

IRIS – International Centre for Women in Photography Established in 1994 at Staffordshire University, Stoke-on-Trent, to coincide with the Signals festival of women photographers, IRIS seeks to locate the work of women photographers within a theoretical framework that extends dialogue and debate beyond cultural, social, geographical and gender boundaries. During the past decade IRIS has attained a reputation for initiating innovative projects surrounding contemporary photographic practice. IRIS has created an educational resource through its membership scheme and aims to disseminate its findings through a wide range of exhibitions, educational projects, publications and new technology. As the only British organisation dedicated to researching contemporary women's photographic practice, IRIS is uniquely placed to contribute diversity to readings surrounding the photograph.

IRIS is now adopting a long-term strategy placing the emphasis on publications offering a particular platform for theory and practice to coexist and contribute new debates and understandings to the ongoing photographic dialogue.

For the Ellipsis publication series we are embarking upon an investigation of the ways in which women negotiate the traditions, conventions and theories accrued around the medium of photography. The series considers contemporary women's practice under the five traditional genres photography has inherited from painting; landscape, portraiture, still life, social realism and the nude.

ellipsis, ellipse, n. Omission from sentence of words needed to complete construction or sense; omission of sentence at end of paragraph; set of three dots etc. indicating such omission. (Oxford Concise Dictionary)

Volume One *Shifting Horizons – Women's Landscape Photography Now* (2000), edited in collaboration with Liz Wells, considered the nature of women's involvement and intervention in landscape photography, resulting in a rejecting of the notion of simple, fixed dichotomies; the essays and photographs propose something more fluid or 'shifting'.

Volume Two *Masquerade – Women's Contemporary Portrait Photography* explores the genre boundaries that define portraiture. Women are operating very productively, and with great success, in the 'in-between' spaces (the ellipsis). The ten portfolios within the publication are the consequence of a selection process that considered over 400 bodies of work. As with any editorial process, this final selection is imbued with our own subjectivity.

We commissioned writers for their expertise, to offer a context for the work through the generation of theoretical and critical debate. These debates will be articulated through the juxtaposition of photographic work and new writing, the idea being that the writing and the photographs are presented as parallel practices, offering multiple and complex readings. It is not our intention to define what portraiture *is*, but perhaps what it *might be*.

Negotiating Difference:
The Transactions of Portraiture

Mark Durden

Many of the photographers and writers in this book both consciously use and subvert the codes and traditions of portraiture in order to raise questions about viewers' assumptions concerning those depicted. One of the recurring features arising from this collection of writings and photographs is the way in which women's contemporary portraiture often foregrounds the psychological and social transactional nature behind the portrait's production. What has tended to have been conventionally and traditionally hidden and gone undiscussed in portraiture, here becomes an important point of focus and reflection.

Take, for example, the disturbing and unsettling series of digital photographs by Alexa Wright, '*I*' (1998-9), as discussed by Rachel Gear in her article examining women photographers' use of photography to create what she refers to as 'narratives of difference'. In Wright's series, the conventions of the stately grandeur of the aristocratic portrait, in which the figure is shown amidst the splendour of his or her wealthy possessions, are radically undermined as the artist deliberately sets up collisions between such settings and the subjects she poses within them. Wright places the bodies of physically disabled women within such luxurious spaces, a display which raises fundamental questions about assumptions of difference and traditional aesthetic hegemonies, the ideal of beauty. The pictures give grace and dignity to bodies which are culturally marginalised, seen as 'beyond

the frame', 'flawed' and 'monstrous'. As Gear points out, such work has its basis in collaboration between the artist and her subjects. This manifests itself as an integral and unsettling aspect of the pictures, collapsing the portrait's premise of a meeting of two subjectivities into one composited single figure: Wright, an able-bodied artist, makes her identification and affiliation iconically explicit as she digitally manipulates the portraits, mapping her own facial features on the bodies of all but one of her subjects.

The full figure colour portraits by Dutch artist Rineke Dijkstra possess something of the frontal formality and harshness more readily associated with anthropological uses of photography. As Jane Fletcher shows in her essay, which considers the resistances and desires of women in both Victorian and contemporary portraits, Dijkstra's graphic colour pictures of naked young mothers holding their newborn babies, with all the visible marks of having given birth, offer counter-idealising variants of the Madonna image. Dijkstra's portraits call attention to the physicality and particularity of individual bodies. But the resultant presence of her subjects resist the reductive and subjugational model ordinarily associated with such a clinical and detailed way of picturing. Fletcher, discussing Dijkstra's portrait of the young mother, *Julie, Den Haag, Netherlands, February 29, 1994*, says it 'achieves a conflation of the earthbound pain of childbearing with a passion that far transcends it'.

One key element here concerns the haptic aspect of such photography, the sense of the corporeal resistance set up by the bodies of Dijkstra's subjects. Gear pays particular attention to this through her essay's consideration of female artists' accent on the physicality of bodies which confront 'contemporary obsession with the thin and nubile youthful body'. Such resistances are manifested, as she shows, in the hyperbolic performative gestures underlying artist Jennifer Saville's photographic self-portraits (made in collaboration with the fashion photographer, Glen Luchford), in which the display of her large body's 'excessive flesh and sensuality' is distorted as pictured pressed up against glass surfaces. Such close up rendition of her own body establishes an embodied seeing, disrupts and unsettles the distance ordinarily set up between viewer and imaged subject. A haptic visuality is also integral to Gear's discussion of the self-portrait depictions of aged bodies by Rosy Martin and Kay Goodridge, pictures which call attention to the potential erotics of such marginalised bodies.

If such use of photography assertively shows and displays bodies which resist ideals of the female body, *Strip No. 6 (Critic)* by Jemima Stehli, as Fletcher shows, confronts the viewer with a more stereotypically erotic female figure. But, by deploying Brechtian strategies, the artist complicates the viewing process. Here males — established critics, writers, curators — are invited to watch and photograph Stehli as she undresses in front of them in a studio setting. Only, in doing so, the scene is photographed, the camera picturing both the male 'photographer' and Stehli. So, the transactional premise of portraiture is here exposed, and the tables turned: viewing is complicated and multiplied, the display of the high-heeled and erotic body of the artist located in a field of differing and conflicting gazes. The plural visual field which Stehli's controlled striptease establishes, scrambles and undoes the voyeuristic gaze.

For Paul Jobling, the generic boundaries of the traditional codes of fashion photography are now much more fluid and uncertain. Beginning with the resistances to and parody of fashion photography set up through Cindy Sherman's staged grotesquery in her colour 'fashion' images of the 1980s, Jobling considers the emergence of a realist look in British fashion photography, focusing on Corinne Day's collaborative portrait of Kate Moss in her untidy flat which spawned the furore over 'heroin chic'. Appropriately, Jobling sets this against the male-dominated fashion world, Day's playful collaboration and intimacy offering 'a deconstruction of the erotic artifice of male fashion photographers like Bailey'.

In contrast to such stylised realist uses of photography, Beth Yarnelle Edwards's *Suburban Dreams* presents a series of tableaux of domestic interiors which hyperbolise the stifling artifice of life in middle-class Californian suburbs. Her hyperreal, phantasmic pictures of happy teenagers, doting parents, in sunny model homes, erase the very realism now so much in fashion.

The snapshot look which characterises Day's fashion photography has become an important code of contemporary photography. Played out as a sign connotative of the authentic and real, it can lose its relation to the particular intimacy and closeness of familial and affiliative looking, which characterises images in the family album. Jane Tormey's close, sensitive and affective reading of the 'ordinary' in photographs by Annelies Strba of her family, looking especially at those of her daughter, Sonja, considers what is at stake in such affiliative looking. Tormey explores the complexity and multi-vocality of this series, taken over a twenty-year period, mixing descriptions of pictures from the viewpoint of the daughter, mother and herself as viewer. This transactional and collaborative, multi-dimensional portraiture goes beyond the conventional strictures of both portraiture and family photography. Strba's informal pictures, bereft of 'irony or cute reference', are seen as unmediated; meaning asserts itself through the insignificant and the ordinary in the image. Dependent on process and relationship, rather than what Tormey calls 'appearance', endurance and duration are integral to this persistent photographic attention, which is 'both diaristic and dialogic'.

Strba's portraits of her daughter find their counterpart in Kathe Kowalski's unsettling series of portraits of her elderly mother. Photographed in the private domestic setting of her home, in states of undress, the mother, playing the role of model to her artist daughter, discloses a second self, as Kowalski puts it, 'immodest and bawdy', in opposition to her public self, always 'very prim and proper'. The pictures' painful performative display functions as a disturbing record of her mother's deterioration as a result of Alzheimer's disease. If the series began with the artist's mother directing her daughter to photograph the tableaux she had created, looking at the final images, harsh and shocking in their disclosure of the aged body of her mother, one gets the sense of someone no longer in control of her self-image and begins to worry about the readiness by which such private displays are readily made public. There is a stripping away of sentiment in these pictures as the loving gaze of the daughter comes up against the painful realities and revelations brought out during her mother's illness.

Catriona Grant offers a series of portrait details of the heads of male youths — mouths, ears, eyes and necks. Her pictures imply intimacy and speak of an affiliative looking. Grant links the pictures' viewpoint with the kind of intimate view to which a parent might have access — only the teenage boys who modelled for her were recruited through a youth club. The subjects remain aloof and self-absorbed. Such images of masculinity contradict assumptions of aggressiveness ordinarily associated with the male teenager. The passivity of these boys at the same time is edged with an uneasy sense of vulnerability, further brought out by the accompanying texts taken from interviews with older men in which they were asked questions about their relationship with a younger male for whom they had responsibility.

Sarah Pucill's staged collaborative performance to camera explores the intimacy and dualities of the lesbian gaze. Proceeding from the artist's interest in 'how the lesbian gaze disrupts traditional psychoanalytic theory that cannot accommodate the simultaneity of identification and desire', her work reveals the resemblance and correspondences between two female subjects, the artist and her partner. In two pictures, one person makes portraits of the other by holding a frame around the other's head, which rests on her shoulder. The contact between the two is tender and intimate. In one image, the framed subject looks back at the viewer, while the 'unframed' woman looks towards her partner. This exchange of looks is swapped over in the second photograph, so that the woman in frame looks towards the other, who now looks out at the viewer. The correspondences and doubling implied by these pictures are further brought out in a third photograph, which shows both women looking into a mirror, tilted in order that we can see their faces reflected in it and understand that each is looking at the reflected image of the other.

In contrast to such reflexive and intimate portrait work as Strba's and Pucill's, Caryn Faure Walker's essay addresses the demotic potential of community or mass portraiture. Faure Walker looks at the formal echo, but fundamental reconfiguration, of nineteenth-century classificationary archival and composite uses of photography, fixated on the face and bodies of the other, with such multi-vocal collective portraiture as Susan Hiller's sound installation archive based upon over 200 witnesses' descriptions of UFOs, or Karin Sander's multi-linguistic *Wordsearch, a Translinguistic Sculpture*, based upon New York residents' donating a single word in their mother tongue which had special significance for them. Sander's democratic and composite word-portrait from New Yorkers — a thesaurus of 48,400 words in 220 different languages, published in *The New York Times* and available on the internet — is far from the implications of the police archives of the nineteenth century, predicated upon a desire to map and visualise alterity. Instead, it shows the

ethical collaborative and participatory process of mass portraiture, especially meaningful and trenchant as the world becomes increasingly and dangerously polarised.

Zineb Sedira's series *Self Portraits* is also of special interest in relation to this. Sedira explores and subverts signs of cultural difference. The portraits show the body completely veiled in a Haïk, the Algerian veil. Combining references to the Christian and Muslim tradition of veiling, and countering the Western media's fixation on the Muslim veil as a monolithic black veil, Sedira's work uses icons and symbols to link rather than separate cultures.

Faure Walker opens out the discussion beyond the conventions of the genre; the diaristic and subjective are effectively countered by a concern with the social and democratic implications of portraiture, a shift from a sense of singularity to one of collectivity. The social and collective historical uses of portraits are integral to the artists discussed by Sandra Matthews. Here, practices integral to extending the photographic portrait seek to unravel the narratives and meanings which lie behind photographs. Matthews is attentive to the cultural specificity of images and their shifts in meaning through appropriation. She begins by examining Alma Lopez's and Delilah Montoya's respective explorations through portraiture of the use of the Christian/Aztec icon of the Virgin of Guadalupe in Chicano (Mexican-American)

culture. Montoya's monumental *La Guadalupana* is based upon collaboration and presents us with a memorial portrait, displayed as an altar, showing a male prisoner, subsequently murdered in jail, whose back is tattooed with the Virgin, symbol of minority Chicano identity and pride. Lopez's digital composite portrait, *Our Lady*, as Matthews puts it, 'allows the Virgin to come down from her pedestal and relate more directly to the viewer, as a strong, beautiful Chicana woman who owns her own body and is not ashamed to show it'. If both work to demythologise a powerful cultural icon, the images of Sheila Pinkel and Meridel Rubenstein, in their respective work with survivors of wars in the predominantly Buddhist countries of Vietnam and Cambodia, give us portraits of specific people as the 'unknowing heroes of myths'. Such artists locate portraiture within history, using the affective charge of portraiture as part of a powerful documentary poetics which provides an important revelation of the personal consequences of wars, long after they are supposedly over. Like so many of the artists discussed and presented in this book, Pinkel and Rubenstein each highlight portraiture's dialogical potential; portraiture here becomes a means of both negotiating and understanding cultural differences.

MAGALI NOUGAREDE

Toeing the Line

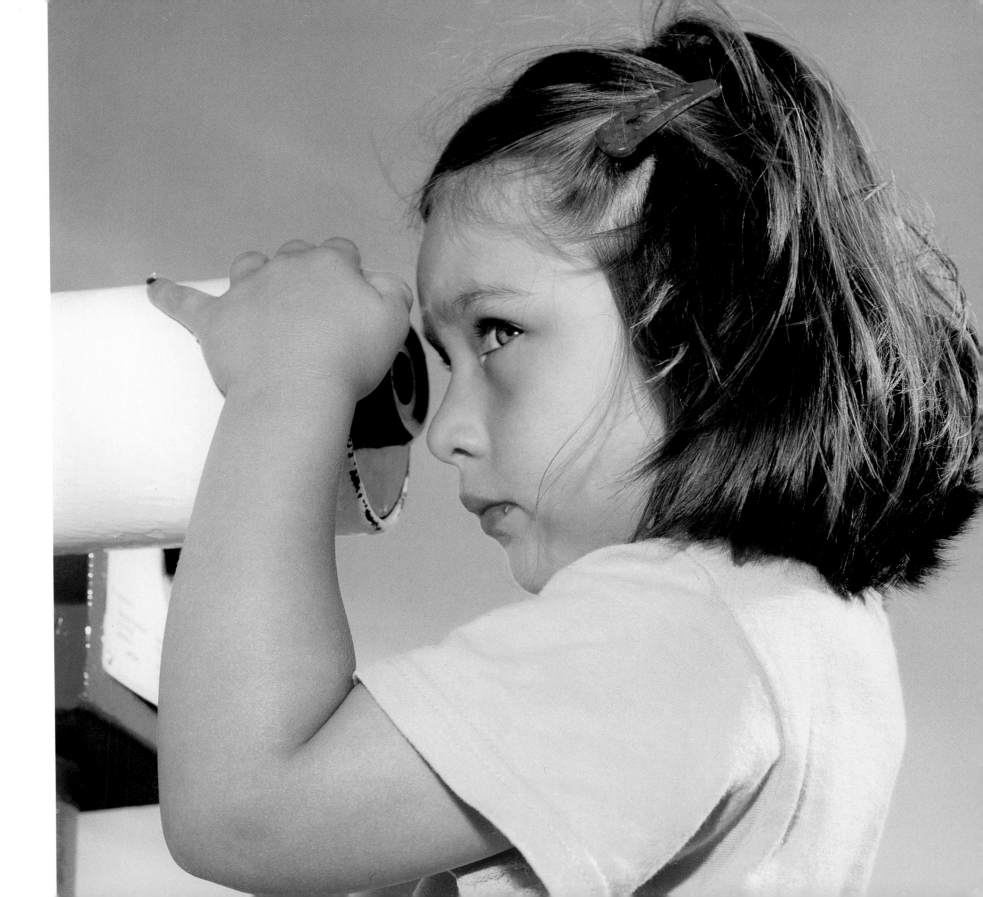

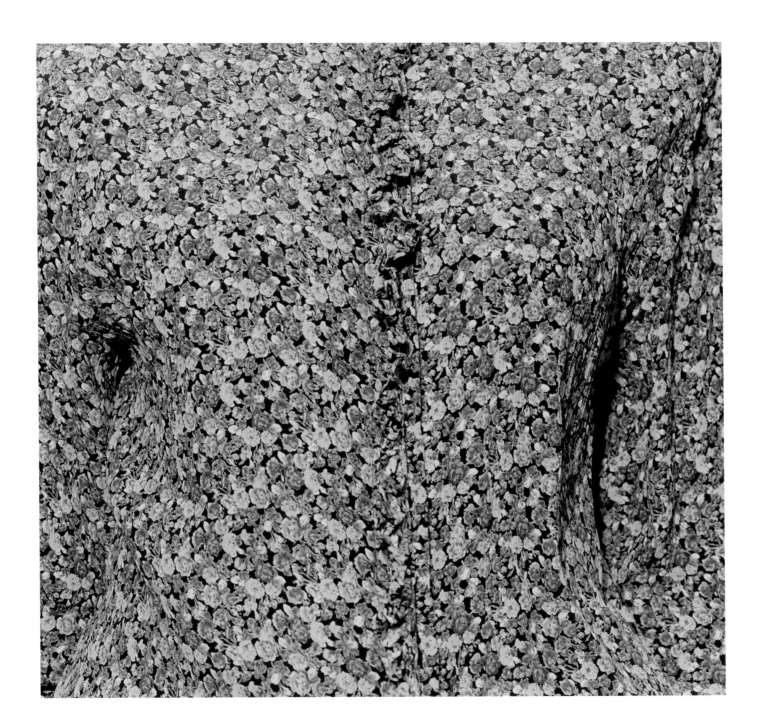

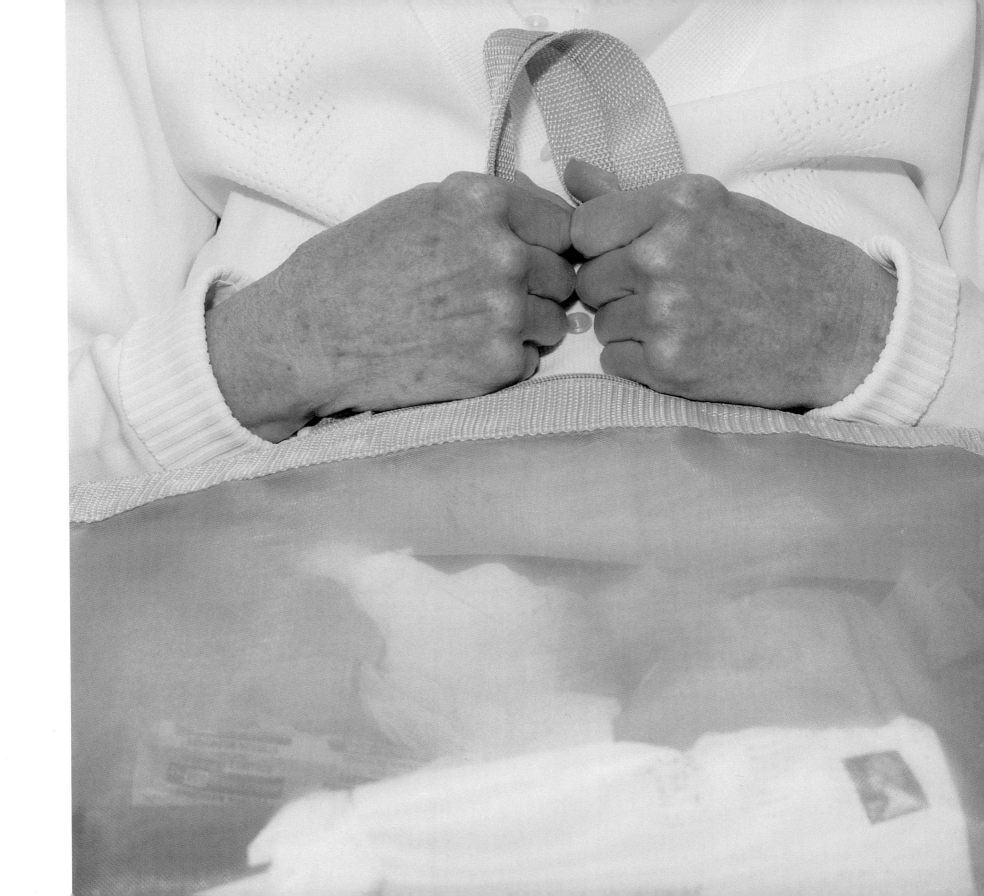

Sonja's Voice:
Telling Strategies of Portrayal

Jane Tormey

Annelies Strba's series of photographs *Shades of Time*[1] presents the detail and singularity of her family over a twenty-year period and Sonja, one of her daughters, features throughout. This series is typical of much contemporary photographic practice in that it appropriates, mixes and subverts traditional genres, in this instance the snapshot and the portrait, and displays an indirect, decentred approach to photographic portraiture. Images of Sonja are described and examined here in order to explore characteristics of Strba's work, such as the qualities of uncertainty, contradiction, marginality; qualities that reflect aspects of debate, which have contributed to a revised approach to the reading of photographs. Roland Barthes, Jacques Derrida and Jean Baudrillard have each written about photographs specifically; have explored how they compel and how we can respond to them. Strba's work provides here an insight into the interrelation between these wider cultural ideas and critical and art practices, besides marking an important development in photographic portraiture. Her method of depiction can be described as diaristic in that it records ordinary day-to-day events, and dialogic in the way the collection as a whole tells of relationships and the nuances of dialogue, as each participant in my interpretation of the photograph speaks: myself as viewer, Strba as photographer, Sonja as subject.

> Sonja is about to pick the glass up or she has just placed the glass down on the surface beside her. Her right arm works as if independently and separately from the intensity of her look, which is serious and focused. She knows that I look at her; her mouth is held together and reminds me of that concentration when looking at oneself in the mirror; when something happens to the mouth and lips; they 'purse'; they pout. She sits in a very relaxed way, sat sideways on a kitchen chair, her left forearm relaxed and resting on the table, her hand dropping down over the edge. Her right hand hovers over the glass. Sonja performs. She adopts a beautiful pose. Or is this my resentful response. I don't have long hair that behaves and looks carefree and beautiful; I don't wear diaphanous and beautiful dresses and pretty bead necklaces. Sonja presents herself, content that she looks like she does. Her mouth performs again — or so I imagine. I am dismissive of this pretty, wistful position. Sonja likes to be wistful. She's interrupted, standing in the kitchen, arms loosely down by her sides, looking at me. She seems to be very separate from the kitchen paraphernalia that is behind her, as she looks intently out and away from it. Her eyebrows are tidy. Her face is almost accusing and confrontational and calm and accepting. She's naked in the bath. She sits on the bed, cradling the cat in her lap. She looks coyly at me in her best dress. She is totally distracted and moving out of the frame.[2]

The genre of the photographic portrait demands more than simple physical likeness and carries with it numerous expectations. Max Kozloff's series of essays defining the portrait provide a survey of assumptions about the function of portraiture: for example, that the subject must be central to the image and that it is the business of photographers to reveal, by means of their special vision, a hidden, indefinable quality that captivates who that subject is. A portrait then, must reveal the person beneath the mask and include qualities beyond appearance, another dimension of 'psychological resonance'.[3] Kozloff states that portraits 'will represent or make statements about people', suggesting that an author's comment is imperative and implying that a portrait must be definitive or should at least strive to be so. An assumption that a remarkable portrait *has* to show character via expression, position and pose has led to very deliberate portrait strategies: portraits that elaborate, 'perform', 'capture' the character, or create a mythic representation[4] or an isolated ironic moment.[5] This desire for character has motivated the prevalence of construction through performance, typified in its extreme form by portraits of celebrities as signs of themselves. Kozloff discusses the 'discreet social and psychological relationship between the subject and the viewer' and the proper distance considered necessary in maintaining clear, distinct positions between the photographer as 'director' and the subject as 'directed' and subsequently 'performer'. The definition of portraiture has been, in a sense, the confirmation of a game, the purpose of which is for the sitter to reveal herself to us.[6] In order to effect this, it is required that the photographer, in seeking to reveal the subject's character, has some 'idea' about the subject, affirming a particular value to meaning, whether it be glamourising, mythologising, authenticating, summarising, as motif or permanent icon,[7] and in so doing determines a meaning already translated by the photographer as author.

A more contemporary understanding of 'portrait' might be one of a 'telling' or narration of one person by another.

Portraiture is no longer constrained by definitions which state that 'any dilution into unselfconscious activity, any immersion within the subject's own time'[8] weakens the 'idea' of portraiture. Instead, the contemporary portrait actively endeavours to use strategies that encourage such 'immersion'. Kozloff again, speaking of Nan Goldin's work, hints at a development in portraiture that 'demonstrates a fluidity of raw contact before any hint of performance rises up to intervene in and conclude the portrait',[9] and indicates a move away from prescriptive, performative portraiture and towards a method where the subject is photographed whilst preoccupied and their attention and involvement is elsewhere. The diaristic approach, and more literally the use of series, are examples of methods which demonstrate a position where the portrait does not remain static but encourages this 'raw contact', encourages a continuing resonance within and between images. Strba's *Shades of Time* moves away from an isolating procedure and provides an example of portraiture, which raises many issues and subverts our expectations of the genre by a number of means: highlighting a literal ordinariness of subject and context, disrupting narrative and special event, rupturing the relationship between author and subject with intimacy, removing the author's 'idea' or vision.

Strba abandons formal posing strategies of portraiture and creates an un-eventful space where the very familiar supersedes the special*ness* of portrayal. The presentation of the individual is simpler, more incidental, functioning more like a diary or a conversation. Neither does she conform to the snapshot entirely, as her single-minded approach over twenty years goes way beyond what may be expected of the family album. Instead, the photographed subject is placed somewhere between intimate exchange with the photographer, the formality of

the photographic shoot and the happy accident that is recognised as a family 'snap'. The series depicts Sonja repetitively, but does not indicate that varied position or circumstance will eventually manufacture the rare and ultimate image or characteristic. Numerous images of Sonja weigh differently; she is questioning, presenting, dejected, preoccupied or concerned. Just as the tone in a voice can weight a statement, so can the direction of these images. Each presentation of Sonja, each version achieved, is fundamental in the exploration of different sides to her visage and character. And, as there is no search for Sonja's essential expression or depiction and as they are repetitive in context, Strba's images speak in different ways, with each encounter, with each spectator. The collection as a whole is dialogic rather than definitive in its method of describing the complex exchange that occurs in every photographic encounter, and specifically Strba's relationship with each of her daughters and their relationship with each other. This is a dialogue that operates internally, wordlessly. It tells no one's complete story and ultimately, because the effect is accumulative, if there is one story then there are many, which are concurrent and divergent, even contradictory. My interpretations, my story can be seen to be implicit in my use of language. Mieke Bal[10] describes interpretation as being interrelated, as being embedded first in the image and then in the language describing the image. Strba's images and my interpretations can describe Sonja in diverse scenarios and in countless ways:

> sitting on the bed with a doll in her lap, looking penetratingly at me, sitting dejectedly at the tea table on her birthday, unreservedly naked to the waist in front of the stove in the corner of the room, sitting alone on a chair displaying the child, combing her sister's hair, preoccupied.

Stories can emerge from the position of the subject photographed, from the position of the one looking at the image and from the position of the photographer.

> 'There are many pictures of my daughter, in which I recognise my mother or myself. I experience this dissolution of boundaries'...[11] She is an extension of myself, she is not a stranger and yet she becomes someone else in the image, no longer a daughter, but Sonja as she prepares herself. Even prepared, she cannot hide everything and she knows that perhaps something unexpected will be revealed. She is between certainty and uncertainty, uncomfortable. As she knows me so well, she trusts me, it is familiar territory but it is still ever so slightly dangerous. She knows that she is being interpreted, being re-presented. In the course of being looked at, her awareness of her own existence alters. At that time she is both in control and out of control, in herself and in suspension for me, in recognising that I am looking at her. She changes herself as I look at her, because I look at her. I construct her 'image' as confirming my sense of her, my feelings towards her, my imagining, for me not for herself, which is not Sonja. Neither image is Sonja. I could construct different ones. My feelings project on to her. They are qualities in myself rather than in her. My feeling towards her constitutes my understanding of her as my daughter.

As these images assume such an easy appropriation of the snapshot as valid portrayal, one might say 'but what is the point or how are they significant?' Their distinctive qualities reside in the fact that they are *not* in themselves special; they highlight the non-speciality of domestic life and of relationships. Because they are so familiar, so ordinary they are recognisable, and because these images do not isolate, determine one story alone or make any point whatever, they can perhaps reflect a more 'normal' presentation of others. They are a collective narrative of the event*lessness* of domestic life. Visibly over the years, the images have become less contrived and more incidental, less distinct from family snapshots. The subjects are not elevated beyond the appearance of what is there; they are ordinariness in the extreme, a celebration of the ordinary, nearly devoid of artistic framing. But unlike the family album, Strba's subjects tend not to smile, are indeed often expressionless, not presented in the manner that normally displays 'happy' moments. She records with studied seriousness and quiet concentration; she does not search, does not frame, does not construct by any deliberate intervention. Strba presents a digressive sequence which does not conform to the logic of time or centrality, yet which inevitably invites, in this context, narrative interpretation in spite of the disruption of linear or fixed reading. Chronology is removed; there is no sequential logic explaining behaviour or location or obvious stories. The emphasis is on Sonja as an individual with whom she lives and relates to in different ways rather than someone in a narrative. And Sonja, as subject, is not always a central focus in the image and is diffused by the degree of insignificant clutter around her. We see this in the countless depictions of her though the years and in different situations, amidst the insistent inclusion of incidental detail and disarray, of bedding, cats, pots and pans, clothing. Each image describes the very particularity of a moment (being, specifically, the detailed quality of a single instance, situation or individual), by positioning insignificant detail around her with equal focus and importance.

Strba sidesteps the oppositional display of 'portraiture' between the photographer and the one photographed, yet still confronts the uncertainty of communication, the elusiveness of direct dialogue, the positional separation between individuals. The nature of confrontation in this instance is grounded in intimacy.

Sonja with Ashi 1988
© Annelies Strba
Courtesy of Frith Street Gallery

There can be no distance between the photographer and the subject, no objectivity, as both roles are confused and blurred by their shared intimacy. It is a subjective diaristic telling of Sonja as it integrates the photographer's, Annelies's, self-reflection.[12] Just as Sonja reveals different aspects of herself, of waiting, playing, acting, removing herself, the photographer, Annelies, might also be changing in response to her subject, Sonja. Simon Morrissey suggests this confrontation to be 'continual competition between photographer and subject for control of the image'.[13] The photographs of Sonja then describe different levels of reciprocal confrontation[14] and conflict between Sonja and her mother. Because she is available to be photographed at any time and frequently, Sonja appears to wait; she is always ready. She visibly moves between acceptance and resentment, ignorance and confrontation. She can be seen to be purposeful, resigned, determined. As she looks at her mother defiantly or submissively, her face changes slightly, imperceptibly for the pose. She steadies herself. She changes herself. In taking the photographs, Strba allows little time for preparation or for the subject to perform a directed character, but creates a small space where the 'subject' can just about determine a position. In giving her this space, she tests the self-conscious and unconscious masks played out in Sonja's demeanour. Sonja is very conscious of herself, her appearance, her image and is rarely caught not aware and nearly always looks at the camera.[15] But because Strba interrupts her and disallows the formal pose, Sonja is not quite able to present a 'theatre',[16] a special version of herself, is not allowed to become what she wants entirely. Sonja is held in a place between pose and non-pose.[17] It is as if she stops momentarily, suspends herself, pausing and allowing the photograph, as if compelled to do so. Sonja illustrates two sorts of relationship reflected in two sorts of presentation: the prepared and the unprepared pose, in relation to herself and the changing relationship with her mother, respectively. She demonstrates an oscillation between the two stances of preparedness and unpreparedness and how, in each, they describe something different in her. She precariously hovers between these two positions as each photograph could so easily be one or the other. She is both at the same time.

Sonja in the Tub 1985
© Annelies Strba
Courtesy of Frith Street Gallery

Here I am; this is what I am doing. Look at me. I am in the bath. I am naked. I am interrupted. This is private. I feel vulnerable. I want to hide myself. My left leg is lifted a little and rests over my right knee. I am nearly covered, but you can see me. I am trying to cover myself, but it is too much effort and I want to please you and I want to display myself. Look at me. I am young. I am perfect. I want to appear as my perfect self. My adult self. My strong self. I do not feel strong. I am interrupted. I am waiting. My hands are open and waiting to hold something. My head is forced uncomfortably forward by the cold back of the bath. I have to look up at you as my head faces down. What do you think you are doing? I am not your child any more. I am as powerful as you. How can I refuse? I want to display myself. I want to hide myself. I am frail. I am vulnerable. Look back at me. I am looking back at you. I will hold your look for as long as you look at me. Take this moment if you can. What can you take from me? It is my moment. I hold it here with me as long as I am looking at you.

Strba's method of immersing herself in the physicality of taking the photograph is pertinent: 'When I push the shutter release, I close my eyes'.[18] She absents herself from any 'special' event, giving what is there to be seen literally no attention, thus denying the intention of

the 'photographic eye' and allowing the intimacy of the relationships and accident to dictate the eventual image. The event is marked by the shutter release alone, the required physical action. Beyond that there is nothing to mark the occasion. Using instinct as strategy, she abandons the notion of the photographer's special vision and renders the special event of portraiture *eventless*. It is both intimate and anonymous. Strba is clearly not driven by observation,[19] but rather the evocation of sensation, of the relationship and what Sonja signifies for her, as mother, rather than Sonja's appearance and what that might signify for others. Strba takes these photographs without calculation; she shuts her eyes; she creates 'a blank region'.[20] Her blind immersion in the situation and her involvement with Sonja remove her as controlling subject, allow Sonja to just be. The photographer's voice disappears as she abandons both control of the image and of interpretation; she herself has 'disappeared' as interpreting subject,[21] as photographer. Strba's avoidance of interpretative staging, of pictorial framing or affirmation of her own 'idea' of the subject, results in Sonja asserting her own idea of herself, her own voice. She avoids the precept of the photographer as author, creating a situation where the photographed subject can become author. It is a method that relinquishes power and a substantial part of the traditional position as photographer, by not preparing images for the viewer and placing more emphasis on the role of the photographed subject. This is a significant turnabout of emphasis, allowing the subject to reassert herself and inverting the responsibility for determining meaning by allocating power to the viewer.

I see her as looking at me, just as she was looking at her mother. My feelings project on to her. They are qualities in myself

Sonja with a Glass 1991
© Annelies Strba
Courtesy of Frith Street Gallery

rather than in her. They constitute the sense for me of her. My feeling towards her constitutes my understanding of her.

The slide presentations and the book entitled *Shades of Time* continue a tradition which originated with Goldin's first showing of the *Ballad of Sexual Dependency* in 1981.[22] Much of the discussion here is equally applicable to the work of Goldin and aspects of others, such as Corinne Day and Bertien van Manen, who similarly use a diaristic approach. Strba's work provides a tighter arena, a more confined context for characters and a more long-standing and obvious intimacy within the family, more specifically associated with the 'snapshot'. Her photographs are less eventful than Goldin's images, less shocking, less prone to accusations of objectification[23] and ultimately more ordinary. Such photographs point to the contradictory contrasts, similarities and confusion between positions of photographer and photographed and the event of confrontation. Both Goldin and Strba involve a struggle between themselves and their 'subjects', and both invite reciprocal confrontation that produces more equality in the construction of the image. Goldin wants them to 'stare back';[24] wants them to actively confront her, resulting in images that betray a shared vulnerability where defiance or resentfulness is barely visible. Strba gets a more complicated response from her daughter, who has a particular investment in her behaviour towards her mother. Strba depicts, over years, a one-to-one struggle of independence and separation. There is an element of flux between performance and non-performance through-out the series, which is not evident in Goldin's work.

Strba's strategy of no authorial comment results in images that are unmediated and not expressive, and which are full of reference to the reality of the situation (for example, the kitchen table) whilst being reduced in obvious meaning. The kitchen table presents neither aesthetic formality nor any obvious significance. Any import of meaning is dependent on the viewer or it remains a secret between the photographer and subject, as it is not shared explicitly. It is not predetermined, trusting in a latent and incidental drama that is always there. There is little aspiration to transcendence or superior vision, or even expression. Strba does not depict Sonja by centring her, in the sense of constructing a personality or finding the profundity in her character through the use of metaphoric reference. Whilst an image with mythic, universal meaning gives immediate satisfaction, it ultimately becomes familiar or even cliché. Dialogic imagery which approaches a sort of meaninglessness, an elusiveness, with little translation by the author, and which is dependent instead on singular individuality and the specific detail of context, may retain a more withstanding resonance. The significance or 'universality' of these images resides in their very detailed singularity and ordinariness. By giving us the ordinary rather than the

Sonja with Samuel-Maria 1995
© Annelies Strba
Courtesy of Frith Street Gallery

extra-ordinary (literally, outside the norm), Strba gives us what is potentially our own experience. They don't offer us any answers; they are not a substitute for experience and are bereft of a directed expression, dilemma or passion. We don't have to have a special eye to see what is there.

Barthes indicates that a translated photographic image, an image already explained by the author, misses the essential and raw import of what is photographed. He suggests that the 'invented' image leaves the viewer no room for response or interpretation because the image is already loaded with obvious meaning.[25] Any expectation of some special quality in a photograph is closely allied to an expectation of the author translating experience, via commentary or metaphor, into some universal meaning. If, to achieve this quality of 'universally true', photographs must signify more generally, must lose particularity, then according to Barthes, they must lose their history,[26] their context and, ultimately, their potential power as images. The specificity of context and the visually insignificant are vital to images if they are to retain an inexplicable rawness, and not be clothed in symbolism or mythic

representation. Barthes repeatedly assigns importance to the role of the insignificant in achieving an indefinable and elusive photographic quality, which he variously described as 'obtuse meaning',[27] 'pure meaning' and 'punctum'.[28] If nothing is left for the viewer to contribute, Barthes' indefinable quality cannot exist and the image is ultimately meaning*less*. Interpretation of Strba's images however, is left with the viewer and is reinvented with each viewer's own reference. Her work, 'without documentary pretensions',[29] doesn't set out to substantiate anything or prove anything. She immerses herself instead in particularity and the context of the insignificant, whereby nothing is translated for us. In the very incidental shots, Strba's images display successive focus of figure and ground as we spotlight every object in the image in turn, as each is of equal significance. If there is purpose, it is for the aspecial moment, the retention of particularity, without irony or cute reference. Metaphoric reference is minimal or indistinguishable.

There is little allusion to other than what is there, little scope to render the subjects as anything beyond themselves. And yet, as Derrida demonstrates, the 'metaphotographic event'[30] is impossible to avoid: what went before; what comes after; what is imagined; metaphor; metonym, is held in each of these ordinary event*less* moments. In reading these images, even the most simple statement 'her right hand hovers over the glass' leads us elsewhere, to what has gone before, to our imagination, penetrating 'the abyss of these metonymies'.[31] The viewer is thus assigned a speaking role which can speculate and position, where 'there is reversibility, irreversibility, diachrony and simultaneity'.[32] Derrida also explores the contradiction and potential inherent in detail that is within the image and additional to the subject, what he calls 'parergon'.[33] This detail or fragment is extrinsic to the representation, but unobtrusive; it is integral but not distinguishable or detachable. He too suggests that the fragment should remain 'discreet' if it is to retain any potency.[34] It is not central to the image, not significant in itself, even irrelevant but the image would be meaningless without 'the glass of water', which is integral to the import of the image as a whole.

Baudrillard's discussion of photography centres around the objective of allowing the depicted subject to strongly emerge rather than the photographer's constructed idea of the subject, thus avoiding 'photography that is aestheticised, calculated and composed'.[35] He advocates that the activity of taking the photograph itself be pivotal, be kept crude and uncontrolled, as an 'objective meditation', 'a mental process',[36] rather than the prospect of the resulting image being in the forefront. Ultimately what he says is that photographs with purposeful intention lose their potential for 'punctum'. What Baudrillard proposes and what Strba's work achieves is that, perversely, in the lack of control or search for intentional meaning, meaning is allowed to assert itself by means of the insignificant and ordinary in the image.

Barthes, Derrida and Baudrillard have each addressed the impossible project of describing the non-determinate or ineffable in their writings on photography. Where Barthes and Baudrillard focus on the indescribable, the elusive and the insignificant, Derrida explains photographic text as being fluid, changing, contradictory and non-determinate. A personal and believable interpretation of reading images derives from Barthes' departure from the logic founded in structuralism and his introduction of a non-definitive logic in his later work,

bringing together the theoretical and the emotional. Derrida extends this reading of photographs in 'Droit de Regards' where, via extreme speculation in his examination of a series of photographs, he explicates 'interminable' narrative as contradicting and challenging our 'desire for stories', just as Strba's images do. His analysis allows every detail to have significance and each participant to have a voice. Derrida steers us away from a definitive account, denying us the certainty of closure, and demonstrates methods of looking and understanding through his questioning of implicit interpretation.

This decentred method is paralleled in strategies of photographic portrayal, such as Strba's, that disturb the reader's expectations, where there is no ultimate image and no end to interpretation. Photographic portrayal in turn, together with an avoidance of a more traditional aesthetic, echoes a corresponding position in critique, explained by Bal as a dialogic approach or 'dynamic process'[37] and by Amelia Jones as 'performative'.[38] Shades of Time holds the contradiction of indiscriminate objectivity and implicit subjectivity in the intimate presentation of one individual by another individual. Construction remains oblique and careless and the emphasis is on superficiality and banality, on simple description. At the same time the photographs employ and rely on subjective elements that are very particular and are dependent on the intimate involvement of the photographer. It is indicative of photographic presentation that displays what is valued now as authentic; it insists on including the incidental and encourages the non-determinate (Derrida); it demonstrates the blurring of impartial and emotional significance, touching objectivity with the subjective

(Barthes) and provokes the emergence of an understanding of the image which is independent of its author (Baudrillard); it questions the 'narrator as the source of information' or as a 'unified voice' (Bal). Strba's work encourages more than one voice. It thereby achieves a fundamental subversion, via conceptual ambiguity rather than a presentation of a literal disturbance using, for example, mechanical devices such as lack of focus or multiple exposures. It is typical in finding a more dialogic strategy to psychological portraiture, having digested traditions of portraiture and the snapshot and modified them. Strba is now profoundly entrenched in another tradition of disregard for a dependency on what is central and unified, replacing it with digressive strategy, decentred vision and a dependency on relationship and process rather than appearance.

ENDNOTES

1   Strba, A., Shades of Time (Baden: Lars Muller Publishers, 1997).

2   Descriptions in italics are mine. The images described are all from the series Shades of Time: Sonja with a Glass 1991, Sonja 1996, Sonja 1984, Sonja in the Bath 1985, Sonja 1983, Sonja with Ashi 1988, Linda and Sonja 1991, Linda with Sonja and Samuel-Maria 1996, Sonja 1977, Sonja's Birthday 1990, Sonja at the Stove 1987, Sonja with Samuel-Maria 1994, Combing Hair 1995.

3   Kozloff, M., 'Variations on a Theme of Portraiture', Aperture 114 (Spring, 1989), pp. 6-15.

4   E.g. Yousuf Karsh's Einstein, 1948, as 'thinker' or John F. Kennedy, 1960, as 'visionary', viewed at Tom Blau Gallery, London, October 2002.

5   E.g. Eve Arnold's Marlene Dietrich, 1952, candid and 'cute' with one shoe off or Peter O'Toole, 1963, caught in the process of fooling around and 'reckless', viewed at Zelda Cheatle Gallery, London, November 2002.

6   Kozloff, M., 'Opaque Disclosures', Art in America (October, 1987), pp. 144-53, 197.

7   Ibid., p. 146.

8   Ibid., p. 146.

9   Kozloff, M., 'Real Faces (1988)', in *Lone Visions, Crowded Frames: essays on photography* (Albuquerque: University of New Mexico Press, 1994), pp. 76-89.

10   Bal, M., 'Seeing Signs', in Cheetham, M., Holly M., and Moxey, K., *The Subjects of Art History: Historical Objects in Contemporary Perspectives* (Cambridge: Cambridge University Press, 1998), p. 79.

11   Strba, A., *Extracts from a conversation between Annelies Strba and Crista Ziegler, April 1998*, (Photographer's Gallery, 1998), www.photonet.org.uk/programme/past/conversation.html, 13 January 2001.

12   Ibid., 'I have to wait for a correspondence between something very internal and something external, as it were. That's why none of the photographs can be completely constructed and none can be a matter of luck, no matter how domestic the scenes are. Often a number of variants of the same story emerge. That's why the process is only concluded with the choice of pictures' (p. 1).

13   Morrissey, S., 'Annelies Strba', *Portfolio*, 29 (1998), p. 71.

14   Baudrillard, J., *Photography or the Writing of Light*, Ctheory (1999), www.ctheory.com, 12 April 2000 'The photographic act as a duel. It is a dare.'

15   Barthes, R., *Camera Lucida* (1980) (London: Vintage, 1993), trans. Richard Howard, published in the USA by Hill & Wang, 1981. See Barthes' playful description of posing when photographed: 'I constitute myself in the whole process of "posing"... I lend myself to the social game, I pose, I know I am posing, I want you to know I am posing' (p. 10).

16   Kozloff, M.,'Open Disclosures', *Art in America* (October, 1987), p. 145.

17   Derrida, J., 'Right of Inspection' ('Droit de Regards', 1985, trans. David Wills), *Art & Text*, 32 (Autumn, 1989), pp. 10-95. See Derrida's deliberate play with words in his description of pose: 'the pose, the position, supposition, the place of each subject'... 'positioning, otherwise called the *pose*...' (p. 25).

18   Strba, *Shades of Time*.

19   Morrissey, 'Annelies Strba', suggests that she creates 'photographs out of relationships' not observation.

20   Baudrillard, J., 'For Illusion isn't the Opposite of Reality', in Wiebel, P., *Photographies 1985-1998 Within the Horizon of the Object, Objects in this Mirror are Closer than they Appear* (Hatje-Cantz, 1999), pp. 128-42.

21   Baudrillard, J., 'The Ecstasy of Photography', in Zurbrugg, N., *Art & Artefact* (London: Sage Publications, 1993), pp. 32-42. Baudrillard refers to the utopian aim of 'disappearing as a subject' in the sense of removing one's own subjectivity or influence in describing something photographically.

22   Goldin, N., *The Ballad of Sexual Dependency* (New York: Aperture Foundation, 1986).

23   See Buchloh's discussion of the possibility of victimisation of the subject in Buchloh, B. H. D., 'Portraits/Genre: Thomas Struth', in *Portraits, Thomas Struth* (Mosel, Munich: Schirmer Art Books, 1998), pp. 150-62.

24   Goldin, *The Ballad of Sexual Dependency*, p. 6.

25   See quotation cited by Shawcross as a translation of 'Photos-chocs', a commentary by Barthes on an exhibition in Shawcross, N., *Roland Barthes on Photography: The Critical Tradition in Perspective* (Gainesville: University Press of Florida, 1997), pp. 3-4.

26   Barthes, R., 'The Great Family of Man' (1957), in *Mythologies* (London: Vintage, 1993), pp. 100-2.

27   Barthes, R., 'The Third Meaning' (1970), in Heath, S. (trans.), *Image, Music, Text* (London: Fontana Press, 1977), pp. 52-68.

28   See his brief logic of 'pure meaning' pp. 34-8 and his discussion of the incidental yet significant object or 'punctum' in Barthes, *Camera Lucida*, pp. 45-59. Parallels can be drawn between Barthes' *pure meaning* and his reference to the *mask* and Baudrillard's allusion to the *mask* as being a more fruitful presentation, rather than trying to get behind it, in 'For Illusion isn't...') Baudrillard also uses the term *literal* in a similar sense to Barthes as having more integrity, being more powerful, in 'It is the Object that Thinks Us' in *Photographies*. Barthes uses *literal* in the sense of bald rawness or *pure meaning*.

29   Rakusa, I., 'Five Approaches to A.S.', in Strba, *Shades of Time*.

30   Derrida, 'Right of Inspection', p. 73.

31   Ibid., p. 70.

32   Ibid., p. 42.

33   Derrida, J., 'Parergon', in *The Truth in Painting* (Chicago: University of Chicago Press, 1987), pp. 37-82.

34   Derrida, 'Right of Inspection'. 'The silent liturgy of the fragment should remain discreet and not give rise to any dream of a general theory, which is another name for the panoptical' (p. 74).

35   Baudrillard, 'The Ecstasy of Photography', p. 35.

36   Ibid., p. 34.

37   Bal, M., 'Seeing Signs', pp. 79-80.

38   Jones, A., 'Art History/Art Criticism: Performing Meaning', in Jones, A., and Stephenson, A., *Performing the Body, Performing the Text* (London & New York: Routledge, 1999), pp. 1-8, 39-50.

BETH YARNELLE EDWARDS

Suburban Dreams

I am fascinated by the signs and symbols of contemporary life. With these photographs, made in middle-class California suburbs, I'm trying to locate the place where the mythic intersects the mundane and where dream merges with reality. Doing this, I'm inspired and influenced by many different things, including genre painting, cinema, performance and installation.

Cathy, age 41
The Toxic Calamity
Colby's Music
The Morning Dash
The Craft Table
Bruce, age 32, and Melissa, age 43
Victory
Going Out

KATHE KOWALSKI

Get Me Some Pills

Rather than live with the constant pain of arthritis, my mother's mother committed suicide in my house, when I was five years old. My father died in 1970. Since that time my mother often thought about her ageing and her dying and expressed her wishes to me each time we were together.

She didn't want to suffer or live in constant pain. She didn't want to be attached to a life-support system. If she couldn't be independent, life was not worth living.

From 1979 until 1991 I photographed her, originally at her suggestion. She had expressed a desire to be my model, as other artists' mothers had been their inspirations. At first she posed for me, directing me to photograph the tableaux she had created. In some of these she was nude or in various states of undress. Although a very prim and proper woman in public, my mother revealed a second self when alone with me, an immodest and bawdy self. The tableaux often described her death fantasies.

When she was healthy I continued to photograph her each time we were together. As her health deteriorated she no longer came to visit me; I went to her. During her last two years I was with her as often as possible.

A year and a half before she died a neurologist diagnosed her symptoms as Alzheimer's disease. As she deteriorated the changes in her came more rapidly. Even though I had seen her the month before, I was astonished by the person she had become. I felt unable to keep pace with her spin toward death. It was all I could do to try to record it. The resulting images, taken during this period, give voice to her final struggle.

There are den children who live in her T.V. room
she says. They eat the candy she leaves
for them.

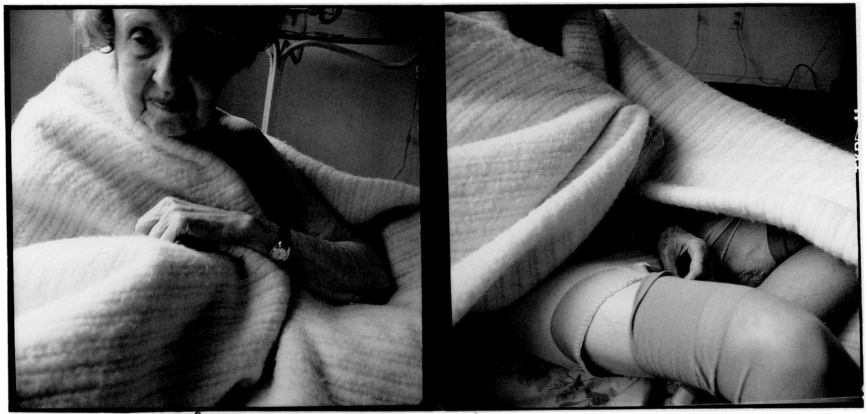

The daughter I never had has become the mother
I used to know.

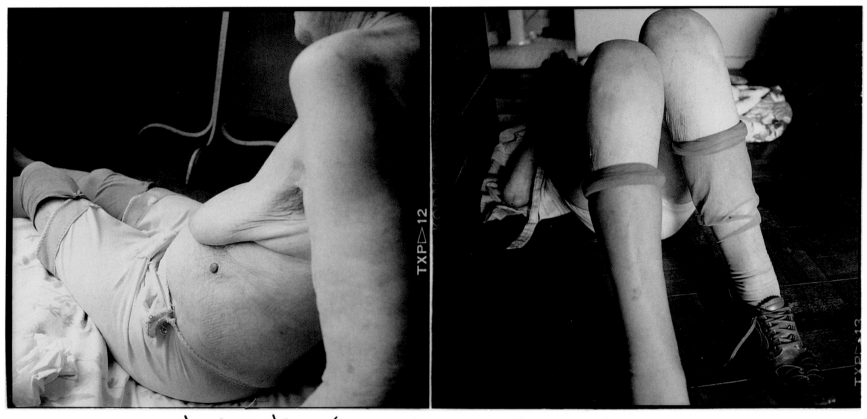

I wake to your screams.

"It's like going to Hell slowly."

Sweet Liberties[1]:
Narratives of Resistance and Desire

Jane Fletcher

This is a narrative of resistance and desire; the threads of the story are strung across the apparently opposing categories of photographer and sitter, viewer and portrait, the past and the present day. Crucially, the inflection of this account is determined by *my* desire to resist photographic theories that reduce the subject of a photographic portrait to the status of mere object, and refuse to acknowledge the potent, albeit transformed, presence of the woman whose image endures beyond the moment when the photograph was 'taken'.

Julia Margaret Cameron's large-scale portraits are mesmerising. The faces appear to thrust their way forward out of the pictorial space of the photographic print. Or, they hover hauntingly like spectres, tremulous traces of what has been. Cameron (1815-79) made her life-size head-shots of men and women in the 1860s and 1870s. She would often annotate them *'From Life'*, indicating that they were not enlargements and — to the initiated — hinting at their long exposure times.[2] Registering the blur of movement, and the detritus caught on the collodion-covered glass plate, her photographs regularly caused consternation amongst the critics, particularly those who believed that 'good' photography was synonymous with sharp-focus and a flawless finish. (Famously, the Victorian photographer Henry Peach Robinson wrote, 'it is not the mission of photography to produce smudges... photography is pre-eminently the art of definition, and when an art departs from its function it is lost.'[3]) But Cameron resisted the attacks of her detractors. Unashamed of the dust, the fingerprints, the hairs, Cameron instead demanded, '[w]hat is focus, and who has a right to say what focus is the legitimate focus?'[4]

Recent, revisionist criticism has required that Cameron be positioned as subversive; a feminist icon in a chauvinistic world of photography history and historiography. Her apparent refusal to be humbled by adverse criticism, combined with her prolific output and inexhaustible ambition, have ensured myriad re-readings and re-evaluations of her extant work and her intentions: some weird, some wonderful. Yet, if Cameron were deliberately subversive it cannot, of course, be proven. That she conceived of her photographic portraits in artistic terms (as opposed to cheap, commercially-manufactured likenesses), was by no means unusual in the amateur photographic circles of the 1860s. Similarly, if her methods of production were unconventional (Gernsheim suggests she 'would impatiently start the exposure before she had focused the image properly'[5]), the results were admired by those who shared her interests and aspirations. As the painter G. F. Watts wrote under one of Cameron's prints: 'I wish I could paint such a picture as this.'[6]

Regardless, however, of whether Cameron consciously challenged conventions, something like 'resistance' resonates through her photographs, and the expressions of the people (the women in particular) who pose for them. In part, of course, this derives from her technique.

The effect of Cameron's working method is most often to soften and diffuse the details of the face, offering instead, a glimpse of something *other than* the minutiae of the epidermis that increasingly characterises large-scale, contemporary photographic portraiture. Helmut Gernsheim calls it the soul.[7] For Lindsay Smith, the way in which Cameron frames her subjects' heads, 'close up to the picture-plane', disrupts the voyeurism implicit in all geometrical perspective.[8] Comparing Charles Dodgson's photographs of young girls with Cameron's female subjects, Smith argues that Cameron eschews the 'depiction of recessional space' that is so necessary and gratifying to the would-be peeping Tom. For Carol Mavor, it is Cameron's conflation of 'person' and 'personification', in which, for instance, Cameron's maid becomes the Madonna, that leads her to argue that the photographs quite literally blur 'the hierarchical distinctions between women', altering the meaning of both in a slippery, unstable, visual and semantic union.[9] Put another way, Cameron's photographs appear to resist a simple description of exterior 'likeness' by making manifest something far more abstract. They resist the fetishisation of the figure by placing her fully and firmly in the foreground. And they resist any attempt to reduce to a stereotype the social identity or physiognomy of the person in front of the camera, by confusing the real with the ideal through role-play and make-believe.

But the palpable 'resistance' of which I speak does not derive merely from Cameron's particular manipulation of the photographic medium (the equipment and the chemicals), nor from the way in which she chooses to frame her subjects.

In a climate of theory that tends to subordinate the sitter to the scrutiny of the surveyor (consider the on-going influence of Laura Mulvey's male gaze and John Tagg's all-encompassing panoptic regime[10]), it is tantalising to discover in the subject — particularly the *female* subject — the potential to resist what is increasingly seen as the inevitable in photographic portraiture: subjugation and objectification. And it is precisely this that Cameron's collaborators, more often than not, manage to achieve. Constantly cooperating with Cameron, her women assume serious expressions and gestures to evoke elaborate names and epithets. Likewise, it is the hypnotic concentration inscribed upon their faces that acts to deny the viewer complete, scopic mastery. Indeed, such is the intensity of their presence that, even when these majestic women avert their gaze, it is difficult not to feel ensnared. Startling and strange, these photographs enthral and enchant. When confronted with Cameron's large-scale portraits of women you are left with the impression that they have *you* in their sights.

On the first of January, 1868, four years after Julia Margaret Cameron scribbled 'my first success' under her portrait of Annie Philpot, another Victorian lady wrote in her private journal,

As dreary a looking day as ever broke on a new year or struck a chill to one's heart on awaking[,] but the band playing merrily on the terrace seemed to say not everything is gloomy "Behind the clouds is the sun still shining" and brighter days will come. The Sutherlands went to Merthyr with us to get our diaries[,]

Album 566, No. 3
R. T. Crawshay
Courtesy of Llyfrgell Genedlaethol Cymru/The National Library of Wales

on returning we all worked at the clothes for poor children. I was taken to be photographed in the afternoon which put me in a bad temper, why do I let it? [T]hough I hate it more than I will tell, and with reason, may it not be a trial sent to teach me to bear patiently what I do not like.[11]

The author was Rose Harriette Crawshay, and she was nineteen and a half years old — to the day.

Rose Harriette was not a happy young woman. Her witty, pretty sister teased her. Her elder brother remained aloof. Her younger brothers plagued her with their petty demands and their nervous energy. Her mother, Rose Mary, made her fretful. There was worse. Rose Harriette had been coerced by her father, Robert, into promising not

to marry in his lifetime. It was something she was learning to regret. In the absence of her mother's affection (Rose Mary preferred philosophy to household management, and was rarely found at home), her father's neediness flattered Rose Harriette. But it cost her dear. As carer and companion to this ailing, irksome man, she increasingly conceived of herself as a captive. In a fit of passionate despair, she exclaimed,

This basest of earthly slavery! How I long to be free. Oh words why do you mock me so. Vain & useless longings, still my heart will not always be cold & passive. It will rebel, & free those chains sometime which forbid its higher flight & drag it, chain it, down to shame and misery. It is a dark hour, may it soon pass...[12]

Robert Thompson Crawshay (1817-79) began photographing in the mid-1860s; he bought a camera and lens from J. H. Dallmeyer in 1866. A year later, he became a member of the Photographic Society of London (which was to become the Royal Photographic Society). In 1872, he was nominated to serve on the Society's Council, along with the likes of Francis Bedford and Valentine Blanchard. Around this time, he built an impressive studio at home, at Cyfarthfa Castle.[13] In 1873 and 1874, Crawshay provided 'munificent' cash prizes for large-scale portraiture, in a bid to encourage 'artistic excellence'. The competition rules caused controversy (and Cameron was subsequently disqualified), but there is little doubt that the Crawshay Prizes inspired debate, and influenced the 'look' of the Society's Annual Exhibitions. When he died in 1879, the photographic press remembered Crawshay for his technical skill, his life-size portraits and his gentlemanly generosity. But, it is from his daughter's diaries that we ascertain Rose Harriette was Crawshay's most frequent, and *most unwilling*, model. Indeed, all that Rose Harriette loathed about her domestic situation – her ambivalence and her anxiety – was embodied in the tense and tedious encounters in the photographic studio between her and her father.

It would be simple, then, to position Rose Harriette as 'victim'; bullied by her father and objectified by his camera's lens. In endless configurations of hierarchical relations, she might easily be positioned as the subordinated *other*: male/female; father/daughter; photographer/model. And yet, Rose Harriette resists her father's artistic vision in various ways – subtle ways and quiet ways – until she finally reneges on her promise, and marries against his will.[14] Her greatest act of resistance, however, is not the ostentatious London wedding. Nor is it the successful attempt to overturn Crawshay's vindictive codicil, which prevented her children from inheriting his wealth. Rather, if ever there were an act of defiance it is that the ninety-year-old Rose Harriette (having first effectively erased any intimacy that she was not prepared to share), gave her diaries to her son to read and preserve.[15] For, in doing so, Rose Harriette ensured that her voice survive the silencing effect of the photographic medium. Indeed, she guaranteed that her voice interrupt and interfere with her father's artistic vision, determining – as it now does, and always will – our interpretation of so many of his photographic portraits.[16]

We know they are sisters, though they hold on to each other like lovers. The one on the right (dressed, probably, in white) rests her hand on the shoulder of the other and peers intensely into her face. She must have moved her head as the photograph was taken, for her profile is soft-edged, and the feather in her cap is a-quiver. Her voluminous skirts press hard against the sepia-tinted garments of her sister. For her part, the figure on the left

wraps her arm around the waist of her younger sibling. Thinner and taller than her paler-garbed counterpart, she stands erect, her height accentuated by an elaborately decorated bonnet. In contrast to her sister, she has turned her head to confront the photographer (and subsequent viewer). And an expression of perfect defiance and anger at being disturbed is inscribed upon her face.

The photograph was taken by Lady Hawarden (1822-65).[17] It depicts two of her daughters, Isabella and Clementina, on the terrace of their South Kensington home.[18] Hawarden first exhibited at the (Royal) Photographic Society in 1863.[19] We do not know what her audience thought of this particular photograph, but its most striking feature must be the displeasure that Isabella conveys in her expression; a displeasure at being interrupted; a displeasure that implies a deep absorption in her partner.

Hawarden exhibited her prints under the titles *Photographic Studies* or *Studies from Life*. There is no clue, then, as to the narrative she had in mind each time she encouraged her daughters to posture and pose. What characterises so many of her photographs, however, is the intimate fascination with which they regard one another.[20] To take another example: Isabella stands before the French windows which open on to their balcony. Her dress is gorgeous, and her hair is beautifully arranged. One hand touches the door frame, the other falls limply by her side. Her back is turned towards us; we cannot see her face. Her mind is on her sister, whom she contemplates, as she bends her long neck forward and tilts her elegant head. Clementina is outside, and wears a hat and coat. One ungloved hand presses against the fixed windowpane, the other lightly touches Isabella's arm through the open door. The glare of bright, natural light (a quality of so

many of Hawarden's photographs) conceals Clementina's face like a gauzy veil, so that her features are diffused, and her brow indistinct. Nevertheless, there is no doubting the direction of her look; her eyes are lifted – martyr-like – to meet her sister's gaze.[21]

Of course, these pictures are 'old'. We might dismiss them as irrelevant manifestations of Victorian sentimentality; ladies of leisure prone to amateur dramatics and affectations of devotion. But, look again and you will see that Hawarden's photographs exude a sensuality that is highly charged and highly erotic. What's more, their relevance remains intact. Full of flirtation and admiration, each amorous exchange played out by her daughters, transcends its historical specificity, speaking lyrically of the fierce fascination we foster, not only for the opposite sex, but always for our own.[22]

And the consequences of these images of love and longing? In what ways do they resist and disrupt the voyeuristic gaze? Such is the power of these pictures, such is the silent wonder that enthrals the pair, that there is little room in the imagination for the proverbial, prowling photographer. The intensity of the sisters' absorption in one another is manifest in every aspect of expression and body-language, and the peculiar effect of this is that their subjectivity cannot be denied. They do *not* exist purely for the pleasure of the viewer. Their desire for one another works to defiantly deny their own objectification. And the viewer can but acknowledge his or her own exclusion, so absolutely do these two young women derive their satisfaction solely from each other.

Through collaboration with the photographer, through determined defiance or through their absorption in one another, these Victorian women variously resist objectification by the camera, the photographer or, even, the contemporary viewer. They force their personalities to the fore. Indeed, the way in which their stories can be retold reveals the limitations of photographic theories that attempt to contain and restrain the female sitter, submitting her — disingenuously — to an omnipotent, omniscient, scopic regime. As in life, so in the photographic encounter, women often wilfully negotiate their own terms — within their own space and the protocol available to them. But, take a quantum leap into the present, and the stakes are raised. The ante's been upped. Women photographers are working within a visual culture that is highly politicised and overtly confrontational. Social mores permit different visual strategies, and nakedness, perhaps paradoxically, has become a provocative — if always problematic — trope for addressing issues of gender and representation.

The Dutch portrait photographer Rineke Dijkstra (b.1959) is best-known for her *Bathers*, a series of profound and sometimes perturbing portraits of adolescents on the beach. Yet, in her continued search for an expression of conflicting emotions, for the experience of 'being', her photographs of post-partum mothers are startling images — at once matter-of-fact and sublime. Though the subjects of these images are vulnerable, there is no sense of violation or exploitation.

Julie, Den Haag, Netherlands, February 29, 1994, depicts a young, handsome woman in a cold-looking corridor. She is naked except for her mesh knickers and a pale-blue sanitary pad. Bare feet on the uncarpeted floor, she stares at the camera, a look of concentration and wonder on her face. The source of amazement is the newborn baby which she holds to her torso: skin on skin. The infant's hair is matted with blood. His arms and legs are smeared with it, too. He appears to wriggle against his

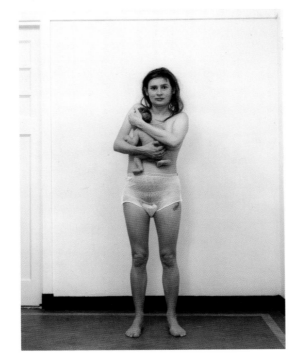

Julie, Den Haag, Netherlands, February 29th, 1994
© Rineke Dijkstra

mother's tilted body, his left arm nudging her breast, while his right leg looks ready to kick. With one hand she cups his bottom, firmly supporting his weight. With the other, she shields his eyes. The gesture is protective, and most likely instinctive. It is also hugely profound. It speaks simultaneously of a touching gentleness and a defiant strength.

Dijkstra's sharply-focused colour photograph makes visible the dry skin on the soles of the woman's feet, and the knotted veins on her shins. The blood on her thighs, and the swelling of her breasts are candidly reproduced in the image. Even the hairs of her eyebrows are clearly discernible. Stylistically, then, this portrait couldn't be further from Cameron's hazy Madonnas. Thematically,

however, Dijkstra's *New Mothers* series echoes Cameron's insistence on making female experience a central aspect of photography. Moreoever, while the fancy allusions and romantic references that define Cameron's photographs have disappeared — Dijkstra provides us with only a first name, the date and place where the photograph was taken — the similarity continues. How? The sympathetic engagement between photographer and sitter is crucial to the success of Cameron *and* Dijkstra. (The power of their photographs depends on it.) Similarly, Dijkstra's attempt to capture the essence of a singular experience and translate it into an image that will consequently resonate with the viewer, parallels Cameron's own photographic efforts to depict something greater than a mere likeness — something abstract yet universal. Thus, not only does Dijkstra's *Julie* evoke the earthbound pain of childbirth, it also demonstrates a maternal passion that far transcends it, a quality most of us recognise, either as children or as parents.

Jemima Stehli (b.1961) is a London-based photographer. Concerned with the representation of the female body, her images occupy a space somewhere between portraiture and performance. In *Strip*, she invites men (art critics, writers, curators) to scrutinise her body as she undresses, and to record the event in a series of still photographs. Male/dressed/photographer versus female/naked/model: there seems to be little room, here, for a radical re-evaluation of sexuality and subjectivity in photographic portraiture. But things are not as simple as they might at first appear. Though Stehli stands and strips, her back is turned to the camera. In contrast, the critic faces it, placed in the spotlight against a bright red background, and holding the shutter-release in his hand. Thus, he takes the photographs while remaining in front of

Strip No. 6 Critic, 2000
© Jemima Stehli
Courtesy Lisson Gallery, London

the camera. That is, he takes them *blind*. Not only is his vision compromised by the fact that he can only guess at what the photographs will reveal, but he is a crucial component of that which he records. In this way, Stehli's studio set-up works to completely confound any simplistic subject/object distinction.

Strip No. 6 (Critic) (2000) depicts Adrian Searle (of the *Guardian*) sitting and watching Stehli, naked but for her high heels. He is on the left of the photograph, and she is on the right. (In fact, Stehli looks as though she has momentarily lost her balance.) There is no denying that she has a 'great' body: long legs, smooth skin and a muscular back. Her 'perfect' physique, combined with the fetishistic connotations of her shiny, black stilettos, seem

to invite voyeurism. But, in this complex field of multiple gazes, Searle is never out of the picture — his expression, his body-language and his carefully-considered apparel. We look at him, looking at her, knowing that he knows we're looking at him, and is squeezing the shutter-release with exactly that knowledge in mind. Indeed, Searle is stuck in the position that John Berger famously attributed to women, turning himself 'into an object and most particularly an object of vision: a sight'.[23] Though Searle might appear cool and collected (note the wry smile, the manner in which he sits), he cannot anticipate the pale slice of his flesh made visible where his sock and trouser-leg part, and which works to unravel his apparent nonchalance. Nor can he have anticipated Stehli's photographed hand — pink and oversized in the foreground — that appears to scratch at his head in a gross, gorilla grope. The effect is ridiculous.

Stehli plays a risky game — a game which depends upon sexual stereotypes and heterosexual ways of seeing. But she challenges the male-gaze, and blurs the theoretical distinction between object and subject, portrait and self-portrait. Moreover, by placing the critic-photographer in a highly-charged situation, she forces him to recognise and register his own vulnerability, and so emphasises the inevitable process of anxious negotiation that characterises any photographic encounter between photographer and sitter. Finally, regardless of who actually takes the photographs, she manages to maintain authorial control — as Rose Harriette Crawshay did in her own peculiar way. Perversely problematic, Stehli's images resist easy narratives of voyeurism and exploitation and, instead, provide a different point of view.

Sally Mann (b.1951) encouraged her children to play up to the camera, as Lady Hawarden encouraged hers.

Emmett, Jessie and Virginia Mann have been immortalised in their mother's photographic landscape, posturing in front of the camera in a series of hallucinatory vignettes, made strange through unexpected juxtapositions of bodies and props.[24] In *The Three Graces* (1994), however, Mann poses *with* her two daughters, recording for posterity a marvellously transgressive act; the three of them standing, naked, peeing in the wilds. *The Three Graces* invokes centuries of feminine stereotyping and female embodiment; in Greek mythology the Graces were personifications of love, charm and beauty. Standing in a line, the Manns' hands touch, and so do their feet. Both Jessie and Virginia bend their heads forward, engrossed in what they are doing. Their mother, in contrast, holds her head high. Her eyes are closed, and on her lips is a curious expression, which might signify ecstasy or a wicked sense of humour. Echoing previous depictions of the classical motif, the central figure (Jessie) in Mann's modern parody has her back to the camera, while the two on either side of her (Mann and her younger daughter, Virginia) face us full-frontally. The photograph is black and white and the tonal range is wide. Strong sunlight illuminates them from the side, so that the contours of their bodies are variously drawn in brilliant white, or cast into smudgy shadow. The depth of field is relatively shallow, so that the focus falls away as the rock, on which they stand, recedes towards the distant horizon — like the back of a giant whale in a vast ocean of hazy grey.

As with many of Mann's images, *The Three Graces* recalls photographic precedents; one thinks, in particular, of Anne W. Brigman's nudes in the landscape. But despite the evening light and the sumptuous textures, the power of *The Three Graces* depends primarily upon the conventions and connotations that it upsets. Whereas the nude outdoors

The Three Graces, 1994
© Sally Mann
Courtesy of Edwynn Houk Gallery, New York

Three Graces exploits the idiom of woman-as-nature, while exposing the culture in which it operates. Indeed, wholly absorbed in the creation of this defiant and provocative portrait, Mann and her daughters speak a daring language of female sensuality and pleasure. Their celebration of the female body is rude and wonderful and totally delightful. Their self-assurance and self-sufficiency make a mockery of the male gaze.

It is a commonplace that every photograph tells a story. In fact, it is *we* who tell stories about photographs. Compelling portraits are productive portraits, allowing the viewer to engage with the photograph, and spin yarns. Tell tales. These narratives need not be of oppression and subordination. Indeed, while it would be disingenuous to discard theories of objectification and surveillance, which continue to be influential because they remain resonant, it is essential to continually revise and re-evaluate historical and theoretical 'givens'. It is essential to endorse the idea of multiple scopic regimes with myriad possibilities, instead of one regime which attempts only to master its subject matter. And it is necessary to remember that the photographic encounter is precisely that — two or more people in some sort of *dialogue* — be it a collaboration or a battle of wills. Two or more people cooperating with, or resisting, one another. Two or more people acting upon different agendas and unarticulated desires. Two or more people absorbed in each other, or turned in on themselves. The women I have described in these portraits are not reduced to objects by the Cyclopean eye of the camera. Rather, I suggest, something of them survives the photographic process. Something of them remains. It is something defiant, something resistant. Something that will not be silenced.[25]

has featured regularly in any history of photography, it has generally worked to reinforce an, albeit shifting, ideology of constraint, one that aligns women with nature. In Mann's image, however, the trappings of culture are boldly inscribed upon their bodies. Pale skin reveals the different cuts of their swimsuits. They wear beads and pendants.

Virginia has her hair in plaits. Conversely, their brazen nakedness, the way they stand with their legs apart and the sheer force with which they urinate, is 'shocking' because it contravenes accepted notions of propriety and femininity — that is to say, it mocks a culture of civilisation that has also succeeded in subordinating women. In this way, *The*

ENDNOTES

1   *The Mountain Nymph, Sweet Liberty* (1866) is the title of a photograph by Julia Margaret Cameron, Harry Ransom Humanities Research Center, Austin, Texas.

2   '[I]n spring 1866 she bought a larger camera taking 15" x 12" plates, fitted with a 22" x 18" "Rapid Rectilinear" lens designed by John Henry Dallmeyer.' Helmut Gernsheim, *Julia Margaret Cameron: Her Life and her Photographic Work* (London: Gordon Fraser, 1975), p. 70.

3   Cited in Carol Mavor, *Pleasures Taken: Performances of Sexuality and Loss in Victorian Photographs* (London: Duke University Press, 1995), pp. 63-4.

4   From a letter to Sir John Herschel, 31 Dec. 1864. See Mavor, *Pleasures Taken*, p. 47.

5   Gernsheim, *Julia Margaret Cameron*, p. 71.

6   See Cameron's *Florence* (1872), Harry Ransom Humanities Research Center, Austin, Texas.

7   'Mrs Cameron had the real artist's faculty of piercing through the outward structure to the very soul of the individual.' Gernsheim, *Julia Margaret Cameron*, p. 84.

8   See Lindsay Smith, 'Further Thoughts on "The Politics of Focus"' in *The Library Chronicle of the University of Texas at Austin*, vol. 26, 4, pp. 13-31.

9   Mavor, *Pleasures Taken*, p. 47.

10   See Laura Mulvey, 'Visual Pleasure and Narrative Cinema' in *Screen*, vol. 16, 3, pp. 6-18, and John Tagg, *The Burden of Representation: Essays on Photographies and Histories* (London: Macmillan, 1998).

11   Diaries 1.1.1868. Rose Harriette's original diaries are locked up until 2062. All quotations are taken from the unpublished transcript held at Cyfarthfa Castle Museum and Art Gallery, Merthyr Tydfil.

12   Diaries 19.1.1869.

13   'The studio situated on the north-west of Cyfarthfa Castle, near the magnificent gardens of Cyfarthfa, is not an ordinary-sized one.' *British Journal of Photography*, 23 May 1879, p. 245.

14   On 5 December 1877, Rose Harriette Crawshay married Arthur J. Williams. Crawshay did not attend the wedding ceremony. Instead, he added a codicil to his will preventing her children from inheriting his bequest to her.

15   Rose Harriette died in 1943, aged 95. Her son, Eliot Crawshay-Williams, transcribed his mother's diaries, and included extracts from them in various (unpublished) manuscripts.

16   For a full account of Crawshay's photographic portraits, and his daughter's diaries, see my doctoral thesis, *The Way She Looks: Robert Thompson Crawshay's Photographic Portraits of his Daughter, Rose Harriette* (University of Derby, 2002).

17   This photograph is reproduced in Virginia Dodier, *Lady Hawarden: Studies from Life, 1857-1864* (London: V&A Publications, 1999), p. 43.

18   They lived at 5, Princes Gardens, London.

19   Two years later, she was dead. Her skill, however, was quickly recognised, and she won medals and praise for her studies and *tableaux*.

20   For an interesting and idiosyncratic account of Hawarden's photographs see Carol Mavor, *Becoming: The Photographs of Clementina, Viscountess Hawarden* (London: Duke University Press, 1999).

21   This photograph is reproduced in Dodier, *Lady Hawarden: Studies from Life*, p. 85.

22   A surprising and contemporary counterpart to this image can be found in William Eggleston, *William Eggleston* (London: Thames and Hudson, 2002), pp. 101-2. It depicts two teenagers on a couch, and was taken in 1974.

23   Berger, John, *Ways of Seeing* (Penguin, 1972), p. 47.

24   Sally Mann's well-known book of black and white photographs, entitled *Immediate Family*, was deemed controversial on account of the way she pictured her children; concern centred primarily upon their frequent and apparently unsettling nakedness. The ensuing debate was complex and convoluted. Mann was accused of many things, including being a 'bad' mother. For a reasoned account of the (cultural) politics in which Mann's images were embroiled, see Anne Higonnet, *Pictures of Innocence: The History and Crisis of Ideal Childhood* (London: Thames and Hudson, 1998).

25   See Walter Benjamin on D. O. Hill and Robert Adamson's portrait of a Newhaven fishwife: 'In photography one encounters something strange and new: in that fishwife from Newhaven who looks at the ground with such relaxed and seductive shame something remains that does not testify merely to the art of the photographer Hill, something that is not to be silenced, something demanding the name of the person who had lived then, who even now is still real and will never entirely perish into *art*.' From 'A Short History of Photography' in Alan Trachtenberg (ed.), *Classic Essays on Photography* (New Haven, CT: Leete's Island Books, 1980), p. 202.

MIRANDA WALKER

Madonna

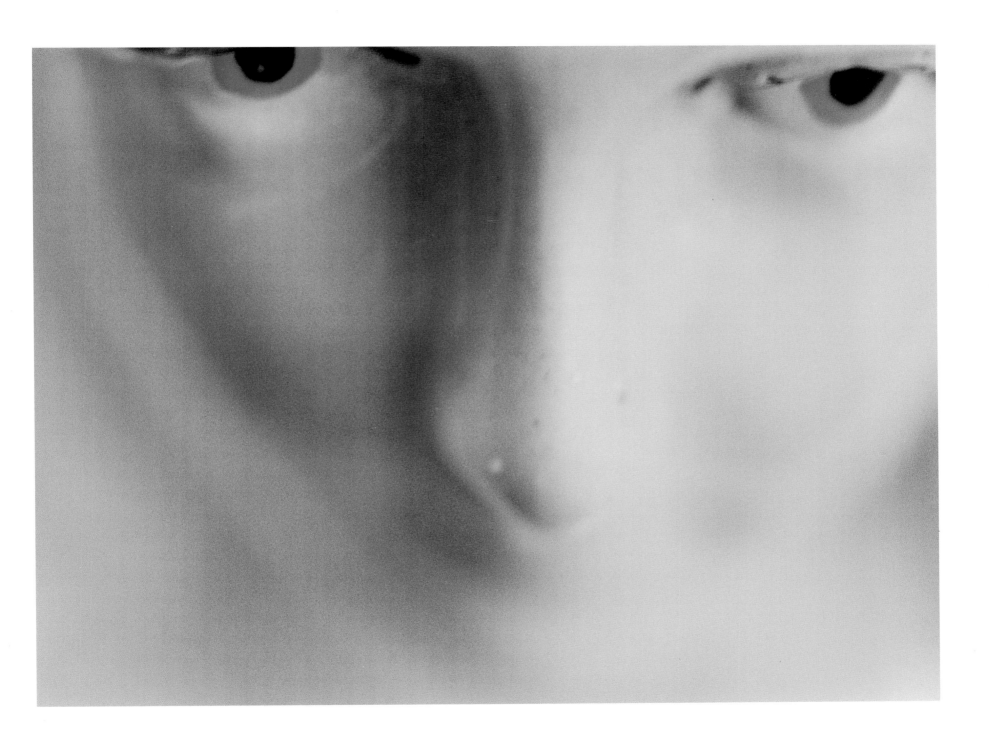

Fashion/Portraiture/Photography: Deconstructing Photo-identities

Dr Paul Jobling

'Body Meets Dress, Dress Meets Body/Body Becomes Dress, Dress becomes Body.' (Rei Kawakubo, The Guardian Weekend, 1 March 1997)

Writing in *The Fashion System* (1967), his seminal study concerning the representation of fashion, Roland Barthes asserts that 'the Fashion photograph is not just any photograph, it bears little relation to the news photograph or to the snapshot, for example; it has its own units and rules; within photographic communication, it forms a specific language which no doubt has its own lexicon and syntax, its own banned or approved "turns of phrase".[1] Certainly, it is easy to agree with such a statement if we consider that many fashion images proclaim a constructed artificiality or theatricality all of their own making, in which the social and political issues of photojournalism, or the provisional and accidental aspects of the family album are nowhere to be seen. Fashion photographer Deborah Turbeville's artful depiction of a wan model, dressed in an evening dress by Ungaro and lying languidly on a chaise longue in a dilapidated salon for the December 1985 issue of American *Vogue*, for instance, conjures up a dreamlike yet strictly controlled mise-en-scène that sides with the otherworldliness of much surrealist practice.

And yet, as Turbeville's artistic approach also demonstrates, it would be myopic to think that fashion photographs are always so discretely recognisable or that they do not overlap with or have anything in common with other photographic discourses. Hence, as Barthes insists, fashion photography is simultaneously self-reflexive and contextual: 'Fashion photographs not only its signifiers... but its signifieds as well'. And it is through this kind of dyadic status that he claims fashion legitimates its own social and economic authority, either by referring to itself in the photographic studio, or to the real world outside the studio, or to a series of cultural and cognitive models such as art, literature and history, which he calls the poetics of clothing.[2]

Nowhere is the formal correspondence between fashion photography and the other sign systems that Barthes refers to more evident than in the representation of human beings, which is to say that the identities of individuals and groups connoted in photographs are as much to do with what clothing they are wearing as with the activities or duties they are performing. By extension this also means that other types of photography can be mined for their latent fashion content, and historians of costume and dress have often resorted to photographic evidence, ranging from anthropological studies to family snapshots, in analysing not just the formal qualities of clothing and dress but their social and cultural meanings as well.[3] Certain documentary photographs, such as Sirkka-Liisa Konttinen's portrayal of working-class communities in the north-east of England, can be seen to function on this level. Many of the portraits included in her photo essay *Byker* (1983), for instance, are revealing of what Pierre

Bourdieu has called 'habitus', the daily doings and things that constitute the social and material existence of groups and individuals, which include prevailing tastes in dress and fashion, evident in Konttinen's portrait of Bay City Rollers' fan Christine Grey, photographed in her bedroom wearing a tartan kilt and striped stockings.[4] Accordingly, in such instances it is often hard to police the boundaries between what constitutes fashion photography and what portraiture, and which issues and themes are legitimate in either case.

The conflation of these stylistic and thematic issues is further compounded in Alison Fitzpatrick's fashion shoot, *Le freak? C'est chic*, which appeared in the monthly style bible *Scene* in February 1999. In a central image from the shoot, the fashion model Christele has been photographed as a Circus Queen who poses alongside her entourage of 'freaks', individuals such as thalidomide victim 'Misty the Lobster Girl' (so-called because her deformed arms resemble pincer-like claws), who earn their living as sideshow and fairground attractions. Along with photographers Nick Knight and Rishad Mistri, Fitzpatrick controversially incorporates the subject of disability into fashion by including portraits of people who, in one way or another, deviate from the idealised body beautiful.[5] Notwithstanding their respective disabilities, however, these people are not objectified as freaks. In the photograph of Misty, for example, she smiles confidently as she poses in a lace and ribbon dress. Moreover, neither she nor the photographer have made any attempt to conceal her deformed arms and, cradled by Christele, who sits behind her like a latter-day Madonna, her assertive gaze seems to proclaim that she has as much right to representation as a glamorous fashion model. That we might not like what we see here, therefore, is beside the point. But what does matter is that such work, whether we regard it as portraiture or fashion imagery, leads us to renegotiate the ethical dimensions of photography, and what we mean by normative identities — in short, the 'banned or approved "turns of phrase"' to which Barthes alludes in *The Fashion System*.

It is with such complexities and correspondences, then, that this essay is concerned, rather than with any notion of fashion imagery as a straightforward entity produced for the sole purpose of promoting or archiving clothes. Thus, mobilising examples of work by contemporary female practitioners, it concentrates on a series of photographic dualisms: namely, the blurring of identities that takes place on one level between fashion photography and portraiture, and on another, the different types of bodies that are represented in them.

One of the most productive ways of dealing with such correspondences and differences, I feel, is to frame them in the spirit of deconstruction and the tactic of the 'double gesture' or 'double writing' that Jacques Derrida raises in his essay 'Signature, Event, Context', through which the classical oppositions of any text or phenomenon are not only reversed but displaced as well.[6] The idea of deconstructive doubling I am referring to here began to take root in the wake of the political and student revolutions of 1968, which sought to dismantle and contest the distinctions between what was inside and outside the system, between freedom and constraint, and high culture and low culture.

It is Derrida who is regarded as the high priest of deconstruction, a reputation resting on a body of writing executed between 1967 and 1977, including *Speech and Phenomena* and *Positions*.[7] His philosophical contribution to the praxis of deconstruction has been to encourage us to move away from, to suspend and to transform the binary oppositions of the Platonic system. In the first place, this involves disrupting the way that spoken language takes priority over the written word and dismantling the concomitant tension between phono-centrism and logocentrism. By the same token, however, it invites us to think more keenly about how we judge things in terms of good versus bad, high culture versus low, subject versus object, male versus female, or black versus white, and to ponder instead the relationship of one term to the other and what he calls the 'spaces' or 'gaps' between them.

Accordingly, as Derrida insists, deconstruction should not just be a matter of inverting oppositions, so as to leave one term always in a position of superiority over another, but should also regard ostensibly oppositional things in terms of relationship, if not equivalence.[8] Hence, he coined the neologism *différance* to sum up the way in which the meaning of any concept is a matter of both difference and deferral, of ruminating on the spaces or gaps between one term and another. He propounds:

> *Différance is a structure and a movement that cannot be conceived on the basis of the opposition presence/absence. Différance is the systematic play of differences, of traces of differences, of the spacing by which elements relate to one another. This spacing is the production, simultaneously active and passive... of intervals, without which the 'full' terms could not signify, could not function.*[9]

Derrida is concerned, therefore, with seeking out what Christopher Norris calls the 'blind spots' of both spoken

language and writing, but his methodology is not without relevance to thinking through the gaps and/or spaces in other forms of representation.[10] In this way he speaks of a general system of writing or representation which he calls 'arche-writing'.[11] And, just as Barthes had expressed reservations about the way that some people believed connotation and the arbitrary nature of sign meant that they could say absolutely whatever they liked about any text, so Derrida was similarly concerned that deconstruction should not become a licence for a free-for-all approach to interpretation.[12] Rather, deconstruction, as he deploys it, is a theory that encourages us to deal with the conflicts and/or contradictions which are already embedded in any text by its producer, and to pay attention to what may be called the marginal details as well as the main ideas in it.[13]

Clearly, deconstruction is a challenging (and often perplexing) theory because it does away with traditional modes of classifying and thinking about culture, and it is because of this that Derrida has sometimes been accused of causing confusion and of encouraging indeterminacy. But in his essay 'Limited Inc.' he refutes this, stating that what is at the heart of deconstruction is the notion of undecidability not indeterminacy, by which he means that we can no longer decide things according to pre-existing, universal laws.[14] Instead, he postulates that what binds us together is a form of collective uncertainty, and the fact that we don't really know exactly how things come about and change. Hence we cannot be expected to have the answers to everything but we have to entertain endless possibilities as to how things can be resolved.

In essence therefore, the idea of undecidability means — to return to the three visual examples cited earlier — that we can no longer claim there is any such thing as a straightforward fashion shoot, portrait, or documentary photograph. This includes what appear to be the most mundane representations of the body wearing clothes. Certainly the representation of clothing and fashion still matters in such instances, but on closer analysis they have to be understood alongside (and not infrequently) in terms of how they relate to other sign systems or forms of representation. Looking at things this way, it would be more accurate to speak of fashion imagery as a series of photographic hybrids or doubles — in the case of Turbeville's image, one that defers and differs the space between high/art and low/commercial cultures and that could be termed simultaneously an 'art-fashion-portrait', or in the case of Konttinen's, one that invites us to ponder just what the boundaries between documentary, portraiture, and fashion photography are meant to be. Moreover, fashion work such as Fitzpatrick's, representing disabled models alongside able-bodied ones, not only appears to double up as reportage or photojournalism, but at the same time provokes us to defer judgement on what is or is not morally acceptable subject matter in fashion imagery.

Probably one of the most well-known female practitioners to have attempted to deconstruct the representation of the body and the meaning of identity in fashion photographs is Cindy Sherman. Sherman was one of a generation of American photographers, including also Robert Mapplethorpe, who embarked on their careers at a time when the politics of liberation, artistic experimentation, and living on the edge had become the norm. Accordingly, the confounding of subject and object positions, as well as the ontological categories of photography, became a central concern for these photographers, whose approach to identities seems to

betray an intense preoccupation with the deconstructive spirit of double-dealing, of breaking rules, and of blurring boundaries and edges.

After graduating from State University College at Buffalo in 1976, Sherman moved to New York City and in 1977 began to use photography to explore the meaning of identity in her series of black and white film stills and series of masquerades and costume dramas, all of which deconstruct female/feminine stereotypes. Although she has claimed that 'I don't realise what I've done until I read what someone has written about me', when we encounter the meticulously staged tableaux in which she appears as actor and produces as photographer, this sounds less than ingenuous.[15] For, without exception, Sherman is both subject and object in relation to her photographs, a performative act that elides the difference between impersonation (this is a part I am playing to try to convince you who I am) and personification (this is who I really feel I am beneath the surface, outside of the photograph). Indeed, in simultaneously adopting the roles of producer and actor, Sherman's work is a trenchant deconstruction of the way that Michel Foucault frames the human body as a crucial site for the exercise and regulation of power, involving those who see yet who are not scrutinised (photographers, spectators), and those who are seen and subjected to 'a principle of compulsory visibility' (fashion models and other represented bodies).[16]

Moreover, her images trade on the idea of the simulacrum, the copy for which no original exists, and on this level too they deconstruct the gap between representation and reality. The most familiar, and probably the most frequently cited, examples of this kind of work are the monochrome *Untitled Film Stills* (1977-80), where

we observe any number of 'Cindys' playing out an array of stereotypical cinematic roles from feisty film-noir heroine to vulnerable career girl. Although we might claim to have some vague recollection of the actual movie characters upon which Sherman's photographic personae are based, as Judith Williamson has observed, the point is that they are not straightforward cribs from specific movie stills at all, but fictions in their own right; the representation of cinematic heroines who never even 'existed' and who we never really saw in the first place, and whose fate we are left to ponder in the condensed narratives of Sherman's non-sequential photographs.[17]

The compositional device of the simulacrum is precisely one that also crops up in Sherman's untitled colour fashion images, which she produced between 1983 and 1984, and subsequent fashion work such as the project for *Harper's Bazaar* (May 1993), and advertising shots for Comme des Garçons in 1993 and 1994.[18] Consequently, in the fashion series Sherman runs the gamut of different model stereotypes, who appear both to parody the excessive and artificial femininity that fashion design and fashion photography frequently dictate and to underscore the reckoning with identity that Barthes envisaged was fundamental to the fashion system: 'We see Fashion "play" with the most serious theme of human consciousness (Who am I?)'.[19] In *Untitled No.119* (1983), for example, she depicts herself in the guise of a confident and exuberant blonde torch-singer, who performs with her arms stretched out wide clad in a navy and white striped top and large anchor-shaped earrings (in turn, decked with pearl necklaces). By contrast, in *Untitled No.138* (1984) Sherman represents herself seated wearing a long black and white striped dress by Dorothée Bis, stretched in an ungainly fashion over her parted knees, matching oversized tie and unflattering mousy wig, as she displays a self-satisfied, imbecilic expression and bloody fingertips. (The image was one of several originally commissioned by French *Vogue* in 1984 but, according to Sherman, they were not published since the editors found them ugly).

Yet Sherman's untitled fashion photographs can no more be regarded as actual fashion photographs, as much as her simulacral film stills cannot simply be taken at face value as representations of specific movie characters. In fact, *Untitled No.119* itself looks as if it could also be a still from a film musical, while *Untitled No.131* (1983) seems to send up the way that fashion photography not infrequently overlaps with 'cheesecake' or pin-up photography. Here, Sherman poses in lace-up lingerie with inverted bra cups by Jean-Paul Gaultier that bears more than a passing resemblance to the fetishistic corset he later designed for Madonna's 'Blonde Ambition Tour' in 1990. At the same time, however, the way that she strikes a coy pout and grasps her crotch protectively, along with the bloodstained fingers and masculine posture of sitting with legs wide apart in *Untitled No.138*, trades on the male subject's fear of castration, and Lacan's idea that phallic power is based on a system of 'having' and 'lacking', which constructs masculinity as active and femininity as passive.[20] Thus the ambiguous masquerade that Sherman performs in both images inverts the normative dynamics of spectatorship and the symbolic role of the female body to be objectified as a phallic mirror image for the exclusive pleasure of the male gaze.[21]

By extension, the use of a vertical format and diffuse chiaroscuro backlighting in fashion work like *Untitled No.123* and *Untitled No.129* (1983) also serves to disavow the power of the linear, geometrical perspective of the male gaze. It is Rosalind Krauss who initially elaborated a penetrating analysis of Sherman's photography on this basis. She argues that in many cases Sherman's use of lighting seems to depict Jacques Lacan's idea of 'the gaze as object à', the luminous gaze through which we encounter the visual, 'not in the straight line, but in the point of light — the point of irradiation, the play of light, fire, the source from which reflections pour forth'.[22] As Krauss contends, therefore, the strongly contrasted play of light and dark in images such as these means that the 'picture is organised not by form but by formlessness', through which both the gaze and the subject are no longer coherently locatable but dispersed and deflected.[23]

In many instances, then, the pictorial codes that Sherman deploys in the fashion series have something in common with her other performative photographic projects. But her images also seem to deconstruct the normative status of the fashion photograph as the harbinger of beauty and perfection, and to disavow Barthes' idea that fashion is quintessentially concerned with the festive on another significant level.[24] Thus in most instances Sherman's clothing is either ill-fitting or worn deliberately in order to make her look awkward,[25] and in several cases she incorporates what the fashion photograph usually seeks to exclude — the ugly, the grotesque, the uncanny. In *Untitled No.137* (1984), for example, she appears with a melancholy downcast gaze, grubby hands and bags under her eyes; in *Untitled No.125* (1983) she has bad teeth; and in *Untitled No.133* (1984) she has flawed skin, and the way that her sweater swamps her torso seems to suggest an anorexic body beneath. In 1990, Sherman essayed a similar assault on the usual codes of fashionable/feminine iconography with her (unpublished) cover design for the American edition of *Cosmopolitan* in which she appeared with smudged make-up and a man's wet shirt stretched over a prosthetic pot belly.

This sense of imperfect beauty is also at the very core of work by Nan Goldin, one of Sherman's contemporaries in America. Although involved with photography from childhood, Goldin's formal introduction to photography came as an art student in Boston in the late 1970s and, like Sherman, she moved to New York City after graduating in 1977. Unlike Sherman's constructed theatre of personae, however, the play-acting that we observe in Goldin's representation of New York transvestites, drug addicts, and HIV/Aids sufferers is uncompromisingly candid and distilled from life in the raw. Many of these photographs, including scenes of post-coital alienation such as *Couple in bed, Chicago* (1977) and drag queens making up such as *Jimmy Paulette and Taboo! in the bathroom NYC* (1991), respectively formed the basis of her projects *The Ballad of Sexual Dependency*, first exhibited and published in 1986, and *The Other Side*, published in 1992.

At the same time, it is interesting to note that, while Goldin's images were not intentionally conceived at the outset as fashion photographs, her brutally iconic documentary approach, depicting unkempt subjects in squalid surroundings, such as *Greer and Robert on the bed, New York City* (1982), was co-opted by many British fashion photographers after 1993 in the name of neo-realism, or what was later to be christened 'heroin chic'.[26] Corinne Day is possibly the most notorious of this new breed of fashion photographer and has openly admitted that her approach to photography was liberated by Goldin's influence. In May 1993 she caused controversy with the fashion spread *Under Exposure* for British *Vogue*, which depicted a scantily-clad Kate Moss modelling various pieces of diaphanous designer underwear in her own untidy flat.

This led several critics, including psychotherapist Susie Orbach, to oppose the work on the basis that it made Moss look 'paedophilic and almost like a junkie'.[27] But this kind of moral criticism seems to take the photographs too much at face value and conveniently overlooks the fact that Moss was actually nineteen years old when the pictures were taken, or that a lack of tidiness does not necessarily connote drug addiction. Like Fitzgerald's representation of disabled subjects, Day and Moss collaborated on the project and, while the images ran counter to the visual codes of the archetypal glamorous *Vogue* shoot, the overall result can hardly be thought of as exploitative or unsympathetic. Nonetheless, the furore that ensued following publication of the spread returns us once again to the central point of this discussion concerning deconstruction and identity: that the difference between fashion and other forms of photography (in this instance, pornography) is not so easy to maintain or to police.

In fact, Day's shoot also disrupts another actual or imputed binary of the orthodox fashion system, that of chauvinist male photographer versus passive female object, and invites us to consider whether female photographers necessarily deal with fashion and identity in significantly different ways to men. Do they, in fact, exercise the same kind of power over their subjects as, say, David Bailey or Helmut Newton?

In comparison to the number of men working in the field, of course, there are relatively few female fashion photographers. *Imperfect Beauty*, held at the Victoria and Albert Museum between September 2000 and March 2001, for example, showcased images by only three women – Day herself, Elaine Constantine and Inez van Lamsweerde –

alongside photographs by ten men (a similar discrepancy is also evident between the number of male and female stylists included in the exhibition).[28] A trawl through the credits of *The Face* and British *Vogue* between 1980 and the present reveals a similar situation and we could once more be forgiven for believing that fashion photography is mostly a man's world. For, in addition to Day, Constantine and van Lamsweerde, we encounter there only a handful of women's names including Annette Aurell, Kate Garner, Melodie McDaniel, Cindy Palmano, Bettina Rheims, Sheila Rock, Nina Schulz, Peggy Sirota, Julie Sleaford, and Ellen Von Unwerth.[29] Moreover, as Day herself attests she had to force art director Phil Bicker to give her a chance at the outset of her career: 'I asked if there were any girl photographers working for *The Face* and he said, "No". I said, "Give me a job, then." I think he thought I was joking: I wasn't'.[30]

A nominal head count like this, however, is not sufficient evidence for arguing that the contribution of women to the field is any less important than that of men since it tells us nothing of the kind of subject matter they are prepared to tackle, which, as the criticism meted out against Day's *Under Exposure* demonstrates, can be every bit as controversial as fashion photography by men. The sense of *différance*, then, between her shoot and those of male photographers lies both in her intention for producing the images and the magazine editor's motives for publication in the first place, so that what seems to be more at stake is the quality of the work in question rather than the more simplistic notion of women photographers being exactly the same as men. Once, when asked how he felt about his relationship with the models he photographed, for example, David Bailey expatiated that, 'They come to believe they actually are like I photograph

them and it gives me a terrific feeling of power. Power and destruction.'[31] In marked contrast, Day had envisaged her shoot as a humorous deconstruction of the erotic artifice of male fashion photographers like Bailey, Newton, or her contemporary Terry Richardson, a way of reclaiming some form of power in objectifying the pleasure that women take in their own bodies, and argued her pictures dealt with the fantasy of 'a sixteen-year-old discovering her sexuality, playing with lacy knickers the way young girls do'.[32] This perspective was amplified by Alexandra Shulman, the editor of British *Vogue*, who openly stated that the whole point of publishing *Under Exposure* was to break the mould of the male photographer, 'shooting a female model wearing black lace lingerie at a hotel dressing table'.[33]

The comments of both women, and the way that Moss is portrayed solipsistically at home in the photographs, therefore, reveal much about the dynamics of spectatorial pleasure, and, in common with Sherman's untitled fashion series, they seem to overlap with Foucault's observation that we are not always just 'docile bodies', waiting to be disciplined by external forces. Consequently he argues that changes in bodily identities — whether they are social, political or sexual — are a matter of internal, self-regulation, of becoming who we want to be, as much as they are to do with external influences: 'Each individual... is his own overseer'.[34]

But, of course, in photographic culture this kind of internal reflection means that we do not necessarily need to resort to images in books, magazines or exhibitions by professionals in order to confront what it means to be simultaneously self and other. On a more mundane level, the viewing and re-viewing of snapshots in the family album proffers this opportunity for self-appraisal, and for negotiating how the meaning of identity can be imbricated with dress. In this regard it is worth recounting the poignant passage in Jean-Paul Sartre's novel *The Age of Reason* where, during a visit to his paramour Marcelle Duffet, the anti-hero Mathieu Delarue becomes curious of a photograph of her taken as a young girl in 1928 that she has recently excavated from her album and placed on the mantelpiece:

He went up to look at it and saw an angular girl, wearing her hair cut like a boy's, and a hard nervous smile. She was dressed in a man's jacket, and flat-heeled shoes...
'I was a scream in those days', she said... 'Such a scream! It was taken in the Luxembourg by a chemistry student. You see the blouse I'm wearing? I'd bought it that very day for a trip to Fontainebleau we had fixed for the following Sunday'...
'Do you regret those days?
'No,' replied Marcelle acidly: 'but I regret the life I might have had.' [35]

In *The Fashion System* Barthes asserts that the reality of fashion lies not in the garments themselves but in the way that they become meaningful through verbal and pictorial forms of rhetoric, claiming that 'without discourse there is no total Fashion, no essential Fashion'.[36] Although Barthes goes on to express a predilection for verbal discourse (what he calls written clothing) over pictures (image-clothing), in Sartre's ekphrastic telling it is the intertextuality of word and image that is pivotal in conveying Marcelle and Mathieu's photographic epiphany and how they realise the way we wear our hair and clothes is bound up with issues of identity.[37] What Marcelle's nostalgic thoughts and Mathieu's sense of estrangement about her appearance suggest here, therefore, is a series of body doubles. First, the idea that we are both the alien or other in the eyes of others and the other in our own eyes. And second, the way that who we —

and who others — think we are is often bound up with appearances, what we wear and why we are wearing it.

Thus the family snapshot, as much as work by well-known photographers, can be interrogated not only for the way in which it appears to contest the ontological categories we deploy to classify photographs but also the way that it blurs what we understand by human identity, representing it as a provisional and dynamic process. Furthermore, like the diverse types of images included in this essay, snapshot portraits are instrumental in the way that they dismantle another fundamental and classic binary opposition — that is the difference between real and imaginary identities proposed by Lacan in his essay 'The Mirror Stage'. Lacan had suggested that one's specular image produces at one and the same time a sense of jubilation and alienation: the former because what one sees in the mirror and in images appears to be a cohesive, fully-formed being, and the latter because the same imaginary being implies a material lack in the actual body, which in comparison to its mirror-image is a body in pieces (*le corps morcelé*). Thus one's ego appears to be perpetually shattered or haunted by the presence/absence of what it desires to become or have: the perfect other.[38] As Sartre deals with it, however, and work by the likes of Sherman, Goldin, Day and Fitzpatrick demonstrates, the photographic mirror image does not always guarantee a more complete or ideal personality, but instead one which is every bit as much a body-in-pieces as the actual bodies we inhabit.

ENDNOTES

1 Barthes, R., *The Fashion System* (1967), trans. M. Ward and R. Howard (Berkeley, CA: University of California Press, 1990), p. 4.

2 Ibid., pp. 240-3.

3 The use of photographs in constructing fashion history is not,

however, my concern in this essay. For a succinct overview of such developments see Taylor, L., *The Study of Dress History* (Manchester: Manchester University Press, 2001), ch. 6, pp. 150-77.

4 Bourdieu, P., *Distinction: A Social Critique of the Judgement of Taste* (1979), trans. R. Nice (London: Routledge, 1984), p. 6.

5 For Knight's photographs see 'Access-able', special issue of *Dazed and Confused* (September, 1988), edited by Alexander McQueen; for Mistri see 'Happy Home' in Flaunt, (August, 2000).

6 Derrida, J., 'Signature, Event, Context', in *Glyph*, vol.1 (Baltimore: Johns Hopkins University Press, 1977), p. 195.

7 The following works by Derrida are instrumental texts concerned with deconstruction: *'Speech and Phenomena' and Other Essays on Husserl's Theory of Signs* (1967), trans. D. B. Allison (Evanston, Ill.: Northwestern University Press, 1973); *Writing and Difference* (1967), trans. Alan Bass (London: Routledge and Kegan Paul, 1978); *Of Grammatology* (1967), trans. Gayatri Chakravorty Spivak (Baltimore: Johns Hopkins University Press, 1976); *Positions* (1972), trans. Alan Bass (London: Athlone Press, 1981); *Dissemination* (1972), trans. Barbara Johnson (London: Athlone Press, 1981); and *Margins of Philosophy* (1972), trans. Alan Bass (Chicago: Chicago University Press, 1982).

8 Derrida, 'Signature, Event, Context', p. 175. 'Deconstruction must, through a double gesture, a double science, a double writing, put into practice a *reversal* of the classical opposition and a general *displacement* of the system. It is on that condition alone that deconstruction will provide the means of intervening in the field of oppositions it criticises'.

9 Derrida, *Positions* (1981), p. 27.

10 Norris, C., *Derrida* (London: Fontana Press, 1987), p. 84.

11 See Derrida, *Of Grammatology* (1976).

12 Barthes, R., *The Elements of Semiology* (1964), trans. A. Laver and C. Smith (New York: Hill and Wang, 1973). In this and other texts such as *The Fashion System* and 'Myth Today' (1956), in *Mythologies* (London: Paladin, 1973), Barthes deals with the arbitrary nature of the sign, but qualifies how far this should be taken by insisting that any act of meaningful decoding should be the outcome of a specific cultural and historical context. Thus in 'The Photographic Message', in S. Sontag (ed.), *Barthes: Selected Writings* (London: Fontana, 1982), p. 207, he argues that, 'the reading of the photograph is (thus) always historical'.

13 Barthes, R., *Camera Lucida* (1980), trans. R. Howard (London:

Flamingo, 1982). The way that he deals with the tension between the *studium* and *punctum* in this essay provides another productive role-model for analysing the relationship between the general message of the text and a more specifically personal one, always evinced by marginal details. Thus he argues that, 'The *studium* is that very wide field of unconcerned desire, of various interest, of inconsequential taste: I like/I don't like' (p. 27), whereas, 'A photograph's *punctum* is that accident which pricks me... A detail overwhelms the entirety of my reading; it is an intense mutation of my interest, a fulguration' (pp. 27 and 49).

14 Derrida, 'Signature, Event, Context' (1977), pp. 162-254.

15 BBC, Arena (1993), 'Cindy Sherman: There's Nobody Here But Me'.

16 Foucault, M., *Discipline and Punish, the Birth of the Prison*, trans. A. Sheridan (New York: Pantheon, 1977), p. 187.

17 Williamson, J., 'Images of 'Woman'', Screen, vol. 24 (November 1983), p. 102: 'The image suggests that there is a particular kind of femininity in the *woman* we see, whereas in fact the femininity is in the image itself, it is the image.'

18 See 'The New Cindy Sherman Collection: The Artist Photographs Herself in a Selection of '93 Spring Designs, Once Again Creating a Cast of Unconventional Characters', *Harper's Bazaar* (May, 1993). The designer outfits that Sherman decided to wear were by Calvin Klein, Jean-Paul Gaultier, Dolce & Gabbana, Vivienne Westwood, Christian Dior, John Galliano, Rifat Ozbek and Philip Treacy. An intelligent analysis of this work is H. Loreck, 'De/constructing Fashion/Fashions of Deconstruction: Cindy Sherman's Fashion Photographs', *Fashion Theory*, vol. 6, 3 (2002), pp. 255-76.

19 Barthes, *The Fashion System*, p. 257.

20 See J. Lacan, *Écrits: A Selection*, trans. A. Sheridan (New York: Norton, 1977), p. 288.

21 Ibid., p 280: 'it is in order to be the phallus... that a woman will reject an essential part of femininity, namely all her attributes in the masquerade'. Laura Mulvey's essay, 'Visual Pleasure and Narrative Cinema' in *Visual and Other Pleasures* (Basingstoke: Macmillan, 1989) has become the (somewhat flawed) *locus classicus* concerning this type of female display and its relationship to male voyeurism. In it she contends, 'In a world ordered by sexual imbalance, pleasure in looking has been split between active/male and passive female. The determining male gaze projects its fantasy on to the female figure which is stylised accordingly' (p. 19). The projective fantasy she refers to here is the result of the male's desire to resolve his castration anxiety by regarding woman as that which he desires to have, the phallus. This somewhat neat exposition of the phallic gaze, however, overlooks the fact that for Lacan it is an 'unapprehensible' ideal that 'issues from all sides', and to which we are all — men as well as women — symbolically subjected. See J. Lacan, *Four Fundamental Concepts of Psychoanalysis*, trans. A. Sheridan (New York: Norton 1978), pp.83 and 84.

22 Lacan, *Four Fundamental Concepts of Psychoanalysis*, p. 94, cited in R. Krauss, *Cindy Sherman 1975-1993* (New York: Rizzoli, 1993), pp. 106 and 108.

23 Krauss, *Cindy Sherman*, pp. 106 and 108.

24 Barthes, *The Fashion System*, p. 250.

25 Speaking of the clothes she was sent for the later *Harper's Bazaar* feature, this is how Sherman summed up her feelings about them: 'Most of the clothes were so tight I couldn't even button them. And the stockings and trousers were too long. But that suited me just fine. It gave the things a non-functional quality; they were already rather theatrical and looked like costumes that have an almost object-like life on their own.' Sherman in 'Cindy Sherman im Gespräch mit Wilfried Dickhoff', Gisela Neven DuMont and Wilfried Dickhoff (eds), *Kunst heute*, 14 (Cologne, 1995), pp. 41-2. Translation by H. Loreck in 'De/constructing Fashion/Fashions of Deconstruction' (2002), p. 273. Loreck aptly argues that this statement reveals how Sherman realised 'costumes as deeply involved in the business of creating identity' (p. 261).

26 See P. Jobling, *Fashion Spreads: word and image in contemporary fashion photography since 1980* (Oxford: Berg, 1999), pp. 2-3 and 112-16, and R. Arnold, 'Heroin Chic', Fashion Theory, vol.3, 3 (1999), pp. 279-96.

27 Jobling, *Fashion Spreads*, p. 113.

28 Cotton, C., *Imperfect Beauty* (London: V&A Publications, 2000). The male photographers, stylists and art directors included for interview in the book are: Marc Ascoli, Fabien Baron, Phil Bicker, Edward Enninful, Simon Foxton, Nick Knight, Glen Luchford, Craig McDean, Vinoodh Matadin, Rankin, Stephane Sednaoui, Nigel Shafran, David Sims, Mario Sorrenti, Juergen Teller and Alex White. Venetia Scott and Melanie Ward are the only two female stylists included, alongside make-up artist Pat McGrath.

29 Jobling, *Fashion Spreads*, Appendix 1, pp. 189-210.

30 Cotton, *Imperfect Beauty*, p. 84.

31 Walker, A., 'The Woman Tamers', *Evening Standard* (23 March 1965).

32 Horsburgh, L., 'Seize the Day', *British Journal of Photography* (8 July 1993), p. 17.

33 Hume, M., 'When fashion is no excuse at all', *Independent* (26 May 1993), p. 22.

34 Gordon, C. (ed.), *Power/Knowledge: Selected Interviews and Other Writings 1972-77 by Michel Foucault* (Brighton: Harvester, 1980), p. 156.

35 Sartre, J. P., *The Age of Reason* (1945), trans. E. Sutton (Harmondsworth: Penguin, 1974), pp. 7-8. The memories triggered by the details of clothing in the photograph in this instance also evince the tension between the *studium* and *punctum* elaborated by Barthes in *Camera Lucida*. See note 13 above.

36 Barthes, *The Fashion System*, p. xi.

37 Ibid., p. 8: 'The choice remains between image-clothing and written (or, more precisely, described) clothing... image-clothing retains one set of values which risks complicating its analysis considerably, i.e. its plastic quality; only written clothing has no practical or aesthetic function... the being of the written garment resides completely in its meaning... written clothing is unencumbered by any parasitic function'. However, the 'verbal representation of visual representation' in the passage by Sartre invokes Mitchell's idea of 'ekphrastic hope' whereby 'we discover a "sense" in which language can do what so many writers have wanted it to do: "to make us see"'. See W. J. T. Mitchell, *Picture Theory* (Chicago: University of Chicago Press, 1994), p. 152.

38 See J. Lacan, 'The Mirror Stage' (1949), in A. Easthope and K. McGowan (eds), *A Critical and Cultural Theory Reader* (Buckingham: Open University Press, 1992), pp. 71-6 and 243-4.

LAURIE LONG

Becoming Nancy Drew

Several years ago I discovered that some of my childhood memories were not of actual events that I experienced but were of events that occurred in Nancy Drew books. 'Becoming Nancy Drew' arose out of the realisation that as a child I had assimilated the character of Nancy Drew — girl detective — into my personality — using her as a blueprint for feminine identity and absorbing some of her fictional experiences as my life experiences. To fully explore this assimilation I physically transformed myself into Nancy and photographed myself as the intrepid girl sleuth, placing myself within a variety of photographic tableaux based on engravings from the books. Each Nancy Drew photograph is paired with a pinhole photograph from the scene and the caption from the original engraving.

Nancy wrote a large SOS backwards on the pane

If only there was enough time to copy the code

The suspect entered the building

"It's a strange message Nancy" the housekeeper said

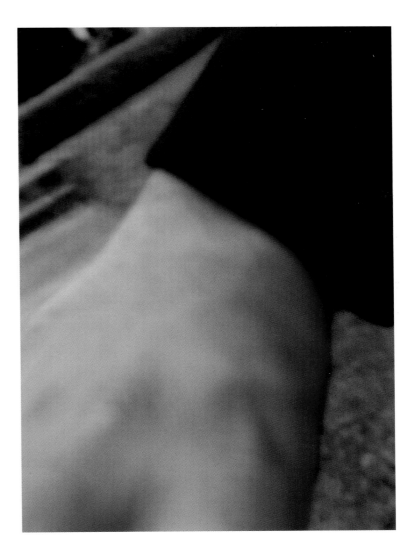

Someone whirled Nancy round and forced her towards the convertible

"Nancy Drew won't get a chance to reveal our scheme!"

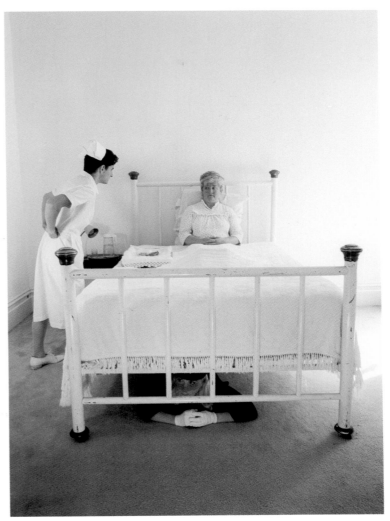

From her hiding place, Nancy strained to hear the patient's reply

MARLA SWEENEY

American Portraits

The Schrade Family, 2001
Giddings Brothers, 1998
Boys, 2002
Locker Room, 2001
Blue Bikini, 2002
Royal, 2002
Justine, 2001

Archiving the Self:
Recent Searches for Identity

Caryn Faure Walker

In *The Body and the Archive*, 1986, photographer Allan Sekula suggests that photographic portraiture remains today heavily influenced by its nineteenth-century functions.[1] They provided a much-needed connective tissue between people in nations where mass migration was prevalent. When pasted into a nineteenth-century window album, and juxtaposed with commercial portraits of famous people, public festivals, civic monuments and landscape views, these portraits also became part of a chronological narrative of how each family 'connected with the outside world of politics, power and pedigree.'[2]

Photographic portraiture was, in addition, used as a means of state control. From the 1840s a new juridical photographic realism became part of a systematic effort to catalogue and regulate the growing urban presence of the underclass. Consequently photographic archives began to contain no longer only the famous and successful, but a shadow archive of the unworthy: the poor, the diseased, the insane, the criminal, the non-white, the female. The demarcation which characterised photographic archives was also implicit in individual photographic portraits. As Sekula notes: 'Every portrait implicitly took its place within a social and moral hierarchy. The *private* moment of sentimental individuation, the look at the frozen gaze-of-the-loved-one, was shadowed by two other more *public* looks: a look up at one's 'betters' and a look down at one's 'inferiors'.'[3]

The most famous of these archives connected to criminal behaviour came into use in Paris in 1872. Invented by Alphonse Bertillon, the system contained a single card for each criminal with a photographic portrait of the individual's face and head taken from the front and in profile. The card which carried this grid of portraits also held anthropometric descriptions and highly standardised notes which supplemented photography's visual description of an individual's face. Cards for the criminal identification system were catalogued to ensure the efficient establishment of two kinds of knowledge: the isolation of a generic 'criminal type' and the ability to convict individual criminals, particularly recidivists.

Bertillon's work on a system that would scientifically define criminal types had been based on previous work in the 1830s and 1840s by Belgian astronomer and statistician, Adolphe Quetelet. Quetelet had attempted to determine a spread of anatomical measurements that would provide a quantitative model of civil society as a whole. At the centre of this model was the 'average man' delineated in statistics. At either side of the average '[d]ivergent measurements tended toward darker regions of monstrosity and biosocial pathology'.[4]

Quetelet compared his work to that of visual artists in search of a likeness of ideal beauty. Sekula supports this belief by finding an analogy to Quetelet's method in Kant's *Critique of Judgement*. Kant writes: 'the imagination can, in all probability, actually though unconsciously let one image glide into another, and thus by the concurrence of several of the same kind come by an average, which serves as the common measure of all... If I am allowed here the analogy of optical presentation, it is the space where the most of them are combined and inside the contour, where the place is illuminated with the most vivid colours, that the *average* is cognisable.'[5]

In parallel to Bertillon and Quetelet, Sir Francis Galton, a cousin of Charles Darwin, was searching for an alternative combined optical-statistical model of society. The result was the quasi-science of eugenics, whose aim it was to assure society's betterment through breeding. As material evidence of his theory, Galton invented a new type of photograph, the composite portrait. Each of these images was the result of the superimposition of empirical data, that is, successive exposure and registration of photographic portraits in front of a copy camera holding a single plate. When completed, these photographs were set out in rows. Composite types appeared flanked by component images. Each such plate illustrated a hereditary type, a medical condition or a criminal type.

About these portraits Sekula concludes, 'In retrospect, the Galtonian composite can be seen as the collapsed version of the archive...'.[6] That is, both archive and individual composite photographic portraits are systems of knowledge represented by: 1) the body of material held in the archive; and 2) by a system of codes on or adjacent to each photograph which include the graphic display of text, image and statistical information. As we make ourselves aware of how these codes currently operate within photographic portraiture, we can begin to free ourselves from remaining unwanted social determinism. We need not be, as D. H. Lawrence has put it, just 'a Kodak snap, in a universal film of snaps'.[7]

Recently this has been attempted via offers of direct participation in making photographic portraits of ourselves. In January 2003 the National Art Collections Fund launched its centenary year celebrations with an exhibition of commissioned works from artists who were asked to reinterpret Old Master paintings. Within the exhibition, the public were invited to create their own self-portrait using a digitally controlled photo-booth situated in the gallery. A person might choose to have his or her face in the disguise of characters in a painting by Rembrandt, Gainsborough, Van Gogh or Julian Opie. Another similar invitation was to take part in *Self Portrait UK*, a project conceived by Media 19 with assistance from Channel 4, The National Portrait Gallery, Northern Arts, and galleries and community organisations in eleven cities throughout the UK. Under its rubric, 'Who are you?', *Self Portrait UK* tempted participants 'to be bold and imaginative, to reveal the real you and present yourself as you really want to be'.

By its mid-February 2003 deadline, *Self Portrait UK* expected to have attracted in excess of 2,000 self-portraits. To stimulate interest in the project, in July 2002 it launched a twelve-month programme with a series of shorts on Channel 4 in which celebrities, such as journalist and broadcaster Jon Snow, disability activist Dr Tom Shakespeare and supermodel Jodie Kidd were seen creating their own self-portraits. What will happen to the large public submission of self-portraits?

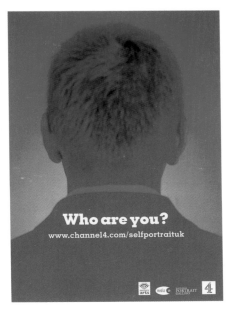

Self Portrait UK (flyer)
© Media 19

According to recent plans,[9] they will be reviewed by three separate groups. Fifty-two will finally be selected: forty to be shown in public sites across the UK and twelve finalists, who will have their self-portraits exhibited at The National Portrait Gallery, the National Museums and Galleries of Wales, and Manchester City Art Gallery. Each finalist will also be the subject of a Channel 4 short.

Belinda Williams, Director of Media 19, considers one of the major functions of *Self Portrait UK* to be 'drawing a portrait of a nation'. Ele Carpenter, the project's curator, sees the genesis of *Self Portrait UK* as being Britain's twentieth-century experiment with Mass Observation. However wide this vision, the organisers have nonetheless set themselves the task of reducing 2,000 plus entries to fifty-two self-portraits. In order to achieve this they must

operate a set of codes to determine the success or failure of individual entries according to the project's stated aims.

Loosely speaking, each selector will apply to his or her process of selection an optical-statistical methodology not wholly dissimilar to that of the nineteenth-century archivists Bertillon and Quetelet. For example, the optical criteria set by *Self Portrait UK* required a diversity of media and for each portrait to be expressive. Their statistical criteria required that selectors underwrote diversity using the measures of 'regional spread... age, disability, ethnicity and gender.'[10] However, *Self Portrait UK* is unable to establish a permanent archive for all self-portraits submitted. The public will therefore be unable to browse or study the entire collection. How can they imagine their own portrait of Britain? And is this important?

To move towards an answer to this question, I would like now to consider work by three individual artists who have also used direct participation as part of photographic portraiture. Helen Sear (b.1955, England) first exhibited in 1980, and has worked directly with the human face since 1998. Since 1969 Susan Hiller (b.1942, USA/England) has been working on collaborative photographic projects using herself and others as subjects. Since 1980 she has also worked with audio and internet portraits of communities. Karin Sander (b.1957, Germany/USA) has been using laser technology and participatory portraiture of communities since 1998.

All these artists work conceptually. Despite being analytic, this process does not aim to evolve identity types. Rather, it is a magnet for emotion and revelation. All three work with paper based photography and new technology: digital manipulation of images, the internet or audio. Sear, Hiller and Sander also share a method of

from the series *Twice... Once*, 1998
© Helen Sear

working in which individual works query what it is we understand through the structure of media. Much of their work does this by juxtaposing the same information in a variety of formats, for example, through a combination of photographs, videos and books.

Sear's, Hiller's and Sander's works prompt us to experience individual and communal identity as multiple and unstable, which theorist Julia Kristeva, in her book *Strangers to Ourselves*, describes thus: 'Henceforth, we know that we are foreigners to ourselves and it is with the help of that sole support that we can attempt to live with others.'[11]

Helen Sear has worked for three years on *Twice... Once* (1998-2001), a series of twenty-eight large black and white archival silver print photographic portraits and large

format, grid-like, digitally produced self-portraits.[12] The series refers to Sear's previous large format C-type prints, *Gone to Earth* (1994),[13] and the artist's digitally manipulated, colour images, *Grounded* (2000-1). Both series are close-ups, in whose foreground are enlarged details of animal carcasses seen against marbled skies. Photographer and writer David Bate aptly describes *Grounded* as virtual landscapes in which 'the infinite space of the sky and the specificity of the body under it, [make] dreams open up. Not the dreams of animals, but the animality of dreams: the unconscious and its sexuality.'[14] This charged atmosphere is also projected by *Twice... Once*. Sear describes the work as 'sculpting in the dark'. This is both a reference to the artist's preference for knowledge rooted in the tactile rather than the visual and also to her distrust of what has been called 'objective' knowledge.

To make the self-portraits Sear hand-holds her camera at arm's length from her face, transfers the image to a computer, and proceeds to dissect her face into a grid of digitally produced, numbered squares. She restores her face by pasting the squares back in order. It is the tension between the hand's re-making and technology's dissection of the image that visibly underlines what Kristeva calls the foreignness of 'ourselves to ourselves'.

Using two different negatives of the same person's face superimposed with an arched gap of space between them, Sear makes a composite portrait in a process not unlike Galton's. The distortions thus produced suggest that identity is malleable, fugitive, ephemeral. The vitality present in Sear's *Gone to Earth* and *Grounded* has been drained from *Twice... Once*. In the latter portraits, blank cavernous eyes and slits of mouths evoke, but refuse connection, between 'I' and 'you'. The familiar becomes unfamiliar in a phenomenon which Sigmund Freud has

from the series *Twice... Once*, 1998
© Helen Sear

called the 'uncanny'.[15] In this pendulum swing the ego shatters to cause inexplicable fear.

Working with collaborative, automatic photo-booth portraiture since 1969, Susan Hiller has pioneered exploration of how imaging technology alters our self-perception, and perception of boundaries between ourselves and what we consider 'real'. Her work has laid the foundation for other artists to use photographic portraiture to move beyond the familiar to the uncanny. Hiller has also been instrumental, via her works of the early 1970s, in the creation of an exemplary model for definition of community, based on what she calls 'group investigations'. Trained as an anthropologist before she became an artist, Hiller has systematically interconnected methodologies of art and anthropology.[16]

Speaking with Stuart Morgan, Hiller describes what drives her to make art: 'We're usually not aware that everything we perceive is a combination of something externally given and something we bring to it so there is never anything without our subjectivity. What I want to make are situations where people are aware that what they're seeing is because of who they are; so they can be

Witness, 2002
© Susan Hiller
Courtesy of Artangel, London

Witness, 2002
© Susan Hiller
Courtesy of Artangel, London

conscious of the fact that they are producing pleasure and pain, that we're not just walking through life as though it were someone else's film. It is like dreaming: you are both inside and outside and it's important to know you're in both places.'[17] The double position inside and outside of dreaming to which Hiller refers has a visual geography in her body of work. To experience this is to be involved in unravelling the coded social typologies inherited by us from nineteenth-century photographic portraiture.

In the *Photomat Portrait* series, from 1969 onwards, Hiller began to collect discarded photomat portraits as she was especially interested in how this technology produced unusual examples when it misfired. In 1972 she was also gathering material for *Sisters of Menon*, in which a multitude of voices were signified by a gestural script which came automatically to Hiller in a form that Surrealists had named 'automatic writing'. The two types of automation, mass-produced photographic imagery and automatic writing Hiller made, collide in these works.

The artist produced eight such series between 1981 and 1983: large format C-type individual photographic portraits; similar images compiled in grids of four or in

unframed large, aluminium mounted, C-type cross shapes.[18] Hiller describes making the portraits: 'I enter the booth with a set of ideas and I loosely rearrange myself in order to carry these out as well as possible. But one has to leave a great deal open as I am working blind and have no control over the unexpected brought about by different focal lengths, lighting, etc., in various photomat booths.'[19] Hiller frequently appears in the portraits, with the outline of her head cut by the photograph's edges; her face tattooed by automatic writing which has later been added to the portrait by hand.

In *Gatwick Suite: Ascent/Flight/Descent* (1983), six images, like Bertillon's nineteenth-century mug-shots, make up the work. Three other images atop this row are enlargements of Hiller's face: facing the camera, eyes closed; her face obscured by her hand; and a profile of her head in shadow, facing away from the camera. The work's title, which refers to the location of the photo-booth where the images were shot, also refers us to dream journeys and mystic experience, an area of deep interest to the artist.

These photographic portraits depict Hiller herself. However she does not refer to them as self-portraits. This would suggest that the images portray something else, a collaboration in which technology on the one hand, and writing-as-drawing on the other evoke layers of reality beyond rational knowledge. Hiller underlines that this experience is open to anyone who wishes to become engaged in such a process when she says: 'I believe thoughts and feelings are collective, not private, that there are social and cultural formations that generate knowledge... Dreams are located somehow just here, in the paradoxical intersection of subjectivity and privacy with socio-cultural determinants.'[20] Occurrence of paranormal phenomena, like dreaming, have long interested

Hiller as indicative of transit between rational and non-rational zones of experience. This is central to Hiller's more recent work, *Witness*, commissioned by Artangel Trust[21] shown first at The Chapel, Golborne Road, West London (2000) and in the same year in *Intelligence* (exhibition curators, Virginia Button and Charles Esche) at the Tate, Millbank (2000). In the installation, over 200 stories of UFO sightings from around the world collected by Hiller inspire the work.

Unlike her early group investigations, this project was realised by the artist working with Artangel Trust and a team of researchers, technical and installation designers. Its central element, the archive of witnesses' descriptions of UFOs, was recorded by actors in each witness's original language and mixed on twelve sound-tracks. A computer programme then generated the voices through over 400 small circular speakers which, when installed, hung from

Karin Sander
Layout *NY Times*: Page C9,
The New York Times, Friday, October 4 2002 (detail)
© Photos Franzy Lamprecht and Hajoe Moderegger

the chapel's second-floor ceiling. At a distance, this forest of headphones gave out a babble of voices. When someone walked among the speakers and selected a headphone, she or he could hear a combination of this babble and a single voice. If participants wished to use the accompanying artist's book, they were able to take in the witnesses' statements at their own pace.

The neighbourhood where the work is sited and the approach to *Witness* through the building in which it stands are an integral experience, comparable to the dream journeys of Hiller's *Photomat Portrait*. Or to the Situationists' *derive*, an intuitively planned *drift* through city space which uncovers hidden meaning; Hiller also knew that the experience of *Witness* would underline the nature of a community where multi-national and English people co-exist.

The structure of *Witness* triggers questions: Who is the witness? What is being witnessed? How is the thing witnessed recorded? With what effect? These are all questions equally appropriate to, and raised by the photographic archives and artists' photographic portraits previously discussed. *Witness* however, suggests another answer: we are participants in a temporary community that the work brings together. This temporary community makes us more consciously aware of the complex mix of London as a melting-pot.

In 2002, Deutsche Bank approached Karin Sander to be the second artist to take part in *Moment*, a programme which asked international artists to create projects of limited duration in the public spaces of different national

capitals. Intrigued by her experience of the lived cultural diversity of New York with which she, as an outsider, had come face to face, the artist decided to take the city and the languages spoken by its inhabitants as a starting point for her project. *Wordsearch, a Translinguistic Sculpture* (2001-2), is a momentary portrait of the people of New York after the events of 11 September 2001.

Like *Wordsearch*, Sander's other work is driven by a number of key concepts. The artist provides the idea for each project and also devises an open-ended process through which this can be realised. Then she steps aside and invites others to complete the work. She says: '[The work] must render something visible that is already present but that has hitherto escaped perception, that exists in a latent state.'[22] What she finds must be of surprise to her and to others.

Between 1998 and 2001, Sander began to work with the

human body on her *3D Scanner* series. Friends and acquaintances, art-world figures and, finally, the public volunteered to be laser scanned by 'a bodyscanner that employ[ed] a 3D photographic process originally developed for the fashion industry. Their data [was] then sent to an extruder, which recreate[d] their body shape as miniature sculptures, slice-by-slice, in plastic.'[23] The infinitely precise eye of the digital camera that scanned each individual carried unique information from each individual, in the form of each person's decision as to his or her attire and pose. Once completed each miniature could be seen within an expanding group of other such sculptures.

As in Hiller's *Witness*, in Sander's *3D Scanner* series our posing and watching others pose is presented through digital technology. That Sander fully understands the quantification of our experience by imaging technology is evident in a new work, first exhibited at the end of 2002, at Gallery D'Amelio Terras, New York. To make *Karin Sander 2002, Portraits by People with the Name Karin Sander* (2002), the artist invited 60 people with the name Karin Sander found in Austrian, German and Swiss telephone directories to submit a favourite photographic portrait of themselves to be included in her exhibition. It was up to those viewing the show to consider whether they wished to draw from these portraits common identity traits amongst the archive of people named 'Karin Sander', or to refuse to do so.

In *Wordsearch, a Translinguistic Sculpture* (2001-2), Sander considers the differences between individuals in New York City and the specifics of their shared diversity through the languages they speak. The work was made available to millions via the internet and in *The New York Times*, to underline the artist's (and others') belief in the richness of melting-pot culture where 'English as a second

Word donors: people giving a word to the *Wordsearch* project
Karin Sander
© Photos Franzy Lamprecht and Hajoe Moderegger

language' is the primary medium of communication.

For *Wordsearch* Sander commissioned two German artist colleagues to go to New York City to ask residents to offer to the project a single word in their mother tongue which had special personal significance. Travelling throughout greater New York, the researchers approached people directly. If they agreed to become a 'word donor', the individual in question would be given a clipboard on which to write his or her word. During this process researchers took a photographic portrait of the donor. After three months the researchers had approached 1,000 people; 220 different words in different languages were accepted for the *Wordsearch* project. Each was then translated into all word-donor languages, resulting in a thesaurus of 48,400 words.

As each photographic portrait of a 'word donor' became available it was flashed up on the *Wordsearch* web site. Alongside it was a brief story about the person and his or her word. In this way the project acquired a visible, chronological dimension. On 29 September 2002 a 61-page colour catalogue for *Wordsearch*, designed by Bruce Mau Design, sponsored by Deutsche Bank, appeared as a supplement to *The New York Times Magazine*. On the following Friday in *The New York Times Business Section*, an eight-page table of the *Wordsearch* thesaurus was printed in the same format as stock-market reports, which normally appeared in the section. One million copies of the newspaper were circulated in New York and Frankfurt.

What is it like to read the *Wordsearch* magazine supplement and use the thesaurus in the paper's Business Section? As a New Yorker myself, *The New York Times* immediately conjures up the city's smells, noise, traffic, its bustle and multitudinous people. Like any national newspaper, it gives off a feeling of being 'fresh off the press', something that must be immediately perused, to be carried around and to be thrown away or recycled.

Unlike the pristine, untouchable quality of a fine art photographic portrait, those in *Wordsearch* in *The New York Times* become special the more they bear the mark of use. The *Wordsearch* catalogue and thesaurus, of course, have other ramifications. The magazine supplement carries wonderful, full-page photographs of New York's streets and buildings emblazoned with a multitude of languages in the form of signs. Also included is a sequence of full-page colour net portraits and stories by word donors. Near the end of the supplement are several pages of colour images of handwritten words from the *Wordsearch* thesaurus. As in Hiller's *Photomat Portrait* series, these seem like hieroglyphs or drawings, handwritten samples of word donors' special marks of identity. Interspersed between these visuals in the *Wordsearch* catalogue are excellent articles and an interview with Sander, giving us an in-depth understanding of the project's context, process and history.

I have not only read the *Wordsearch* supplement, but have also browsed many times through its eight-page thesaurus of 48,400 words. Stymied at first by the sheer number of languages I didn't understand, or even knew existed, I began to make my way into its densely woven linguistic cross-references. In the privacy of my workroom, it was exciting to discover that among this group of speakers, not only did 'Joe' and 'John' speak different languages, but 'word donors' who bear the same name, the 'Hannahs' and 'Fatimas', etc., are also multilingual.

For Sander the thesaurus has 'strong', universal words, like 'mother', 'bread' or 'house', and 'weak' words, like 'computer', 'online' or 'hi-fi', which are used across cultures without change. For me, the occurrence of other words — 'guest', 'mirror', 'body' — intimate that most of us sense, or at least want to imagine, how to build bridges between ourselves and those overtly different from us in appearance and/or lifestyle. What has also impressed me in thinking about photographic portraiture in this regard is that, although inclusion of the widest circle of people is essential to democratic shaping of individual and communal identities via photography, this process only becomes effective at the point when we invite face-to-face engagement with others.

ENDNOTES

1   Sekula, Allan, 'The Body and the Archive', in *October*, vol. 39 (Cambridge, Massachusetts: MIT Press, 1986), p. 7.

2   Chambers, Deborah, 'Family as Place: Family Photographic Albums and the Domestication of Public and Private Space', in Joan M. Schwartz and James R. Ryan (eds), *Picturing Place, Photography and the Geographical Imagination* (London: I. B. Tauris, 2003), p. 99.

3   Sekula, 'The Body and the Archive', p. 7.

4   Sekula, 'The Body and the Archive', p. 22.

5   Kant, Immanuel, *Critique of Judgement*, trans. J. H. Bernard (London: Macmillan, 1914), pp. 87-8, quoted in Sekula, 'The Body and the Archive', n. 38, p. 23.

6   Kant, *Critique of Judgement*, p. 54.

7   Lawrence, D. H., 'Art and Morality', in *Calender of Modern Letters*, November, 1925, as quoted in Chevrier, Jean-François, 'The Image of the Other', in *Staging the Self, Self-Portrait Photography 1840s-1980s* (London, Plymouth: National Portrait Gallery/Plymouth Art Centre, 1987), p. 12.

8   Media 19, undated press release for *Self-Portrait UK*.

9   Media 19, 2nd draft: *Self-Portrait UK* Selection Process, 2003, unpublished briefing paper.

10 Ibid.

11 Kristeva, Julia, *Strangers to Ourselves*, trans. Leon C. Roudiez (New York: Columbia University Press), p. 170, quoted in Royle, Nicholas, *The Uncanny* (Manchester: Manchester University Press, 2003), p. 7.

12 Shown in England and Sweden (Prue O'Day, London: 1998; Angel Row, Nottingham, 1999; and Zinc Gallery, Stockholm, 2000). A number of the black and white portraits were subsequently published in Sear, Helen, Morris, Sharon, Bate, David, and Kent, Liz, *Twice* (London: Zelda Cheatle Press, 2002).

13 See my article on Sear's work, 'Spellbound: New Photographs by Helen Sear', in *Portfolio, the catalogue of contemporary photography in britain*, 22 (Edinburgh: Portfolio Gallery, 1995).

14 Sear et al., *Twice*, unpaginated.

15 Freud, Sigmund, 'The Uncanny' (1919), in *Pelican Freud Library*, 14, trans. James Strachey (Harmondsworth: Penguin, 1985), pp. 335-76.

16 For detailed chronologies of Susan Hiller's body of work between 1969 and 1996 see the following: Hiller, Susan (ed. Barbara Einzig, introduction, Lucy Lippard), *Thinking about Art* (Manchester: Manchester University Press, 1996); and Brett, Guy, Bradley, Fiona, and Morgan, Stuart, *Susan Hiller* (Liverpool: Tate Gallery, 1996).

17 Morgan, Stuart, 'Beyond Control', an interview with Susan Hiller, in Brett et al., *Susan Hiller*, p. 44 (reprinted by permission of *Frieze 23*, Summer 1995).

18 The complete series includes: *Sometimes I think I'm a Verb instead of a Pronoun* (1981-2), *Bad Dreams* (1981-3), *Lucid Dreams* (1982), *Photomat (Self-) Portraits* (1982), *Midnight, Euston* (1982), *Midnight, Tottenham Court Road* (1982), *Midnight Baker Street* (1983) and *Gatwick Suite: Ascent/Flight/Descent* (1983).

19 'Portrait of the Artist as a Photomat' in *Thinking About Art, Conversations with Susan Hiller*, p. 61.

20 'Portrait of the Artist as a Photomat', p. 123.

21 I would like to thank James Lingwood and Nina at Artangel Trust and the librarians at Hyman Kreitman Research Centre, Tate, Millbank, for their help in giving me access to each institution's archived material on Susan Hiller.

22 Welzer, Harald, and Sander, Karin, 'On Making Things Visible', A Conversation. http://www.karinsander.de/en/interview.html, 1 Jan 2002.

23 Sander, Karin, in *Karin Sander*, catalogue to exhibition (Stuttgart: Stattsgalerie, Hatje Cantz, Ostifldern-Ruit, 2002), p. 97.

CATRIONA GRANT

Role Models

My working practice involves groups of individuals who have acted as models, actors or collaborators. *Role Models* is a piece of social commentary; it is not a documentary piece, and the young men who modelled were recruited through a youth club. Their role in the making is determined by my intentions for the work and by negotiation with the prospective participants. I am interested in relationships: between individuals; within groups of people; between the individual and the institution.

Role Models, shown as a series of digital, colour photographic prints with accompanying texts, is a piece about young men — their influences, where and to whom they look for their inspiration and guidance, the prejudicial manner in which they are often portrayed and perceived. The boys do not make eye contact with the camera/viewer. They appear self-contained, either contemplative or bored and disengaged from their surroundings. Their portraits show the delicate skin at the ear, the mouth, the neck; these are the kind of viewpoints to which a parent might have access. Seen in this intimate and compassionate manner, the boys are allowed a kind of vulnerability denied them by the popular conception of the teenage boy as troublemaker and by the pressure to conform within their peer group.

The texts accompanying the images are taken from interviews with older men in which they were asked questions about their relationship with a younger male for whom they had responsibility. They talk about love, friendship, companionship, but also about the power structure of the relationship, the speaker being the dominant partner in each relationship.

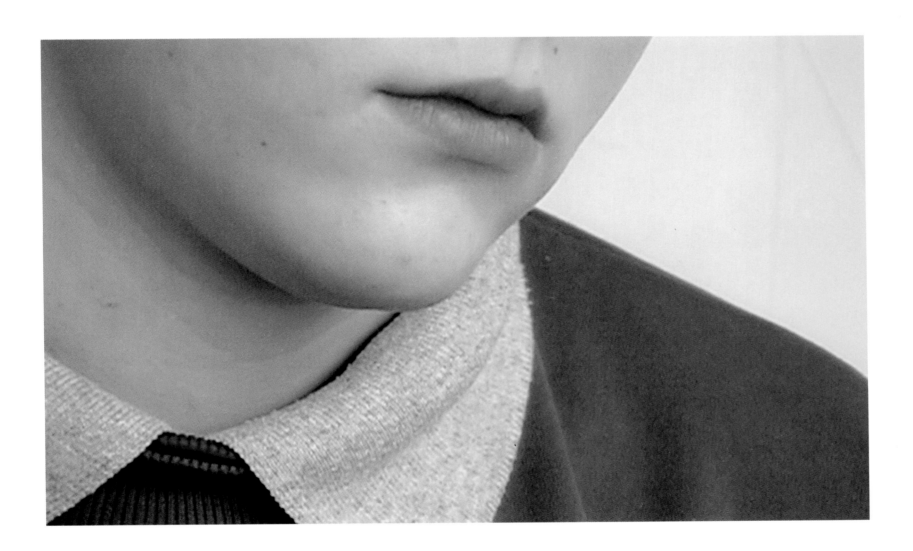

I'm still the person that he looks up to most,
the person probably that he trusts most in many ways

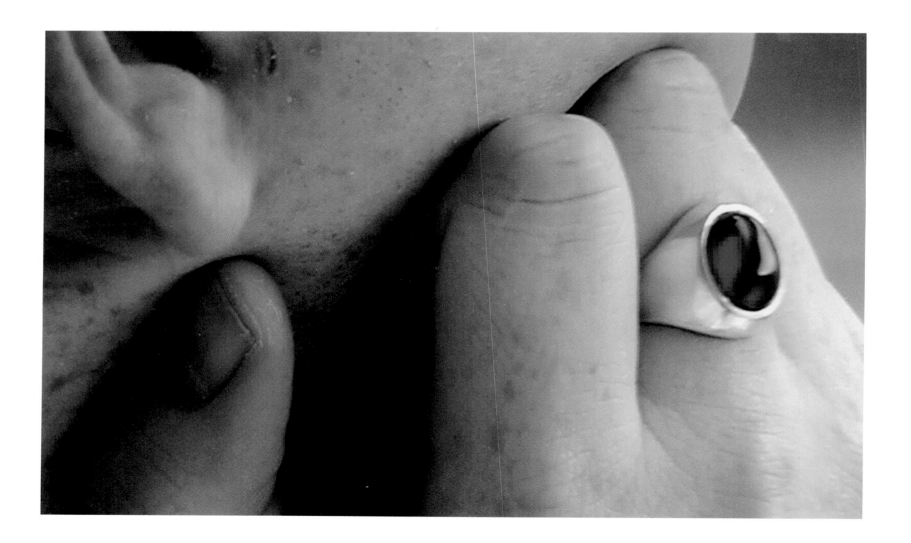

He never competes with me in any way, he just accepts that I'm the boss

He never picks on anyone, no. I've never seen him being aggressive
to anyone through boredom or for any reason at all

It's really quite hard to put into words what I feel about him.
I think he knows that I care for him and he cares for me

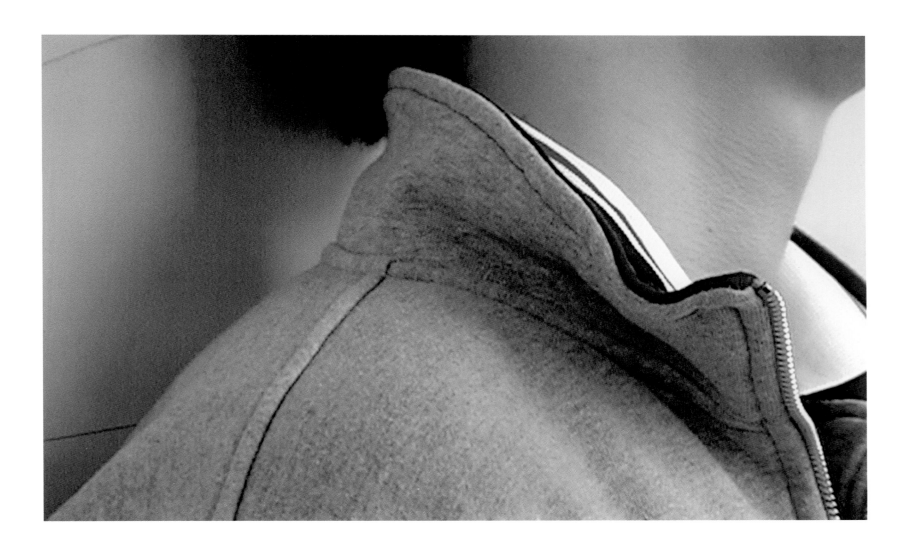

I think he loves me, you know. I think that's how he feels about me anyway

SARAH PUCILL

I have been interested in how the lesbian gaze disrupts traditional psychoanalytic theory that cannot accommodate the simultaneity of identification and desire. Between desire and identification what is self and other is blurred. There is a duality inherent in the lesbian gaze where looking and being seen are not divided across gender lines (as a result of dominant cultural codes and conditioning). The images play with the idea that being and seeing mean being in two places at the same time.

Whilst the images are posed, there is nevertheless a biographical subtext to the work where a relationship between loving and looking is inextricable from the staging of the pose.

We hold the mirror up for the viewer who is also us, to bear these multiple crossroads of joins and splits in subjectivity.

Beyond the Frame:
Narratives of Otherness

Rachel Gear

Contemporary women photographers have sought to use the camera to create narratives of difference that are rooted in female experience, identity and corporeality. Their strategies for doing so have included phototherapy, digital imaging, performance and masquerade. This essay will discuss the work of a number of contemporary women artists who use the trope of self-portraiture in their photographic exploration of bodies that are traditionally 'beyond the frame'. The representation of the ageing female body, the disabled body and the monstrous body will be central to the discussion, as will notions of collaboration and the interface between text and image. Recent feminist theory offers a productive strategy through which to think about such works; for example, the notion of haptic visuality, as developed by Laura Marks in relation to intercultural cinema, is particularly useful in developing a deeper understanding of what it means to view self-portraiture that is rooted in corporeality. This mode of viewing moves towards the concept of a more tactile and embodied viewing of artworks where boundaries and differences become blurred.

In the history of Western art, the older woman is virtually absent. Traditionally, the rigid aesthetic borders that govern what is acceptable and unacceptable in art have placed the ageing body outside the frame; only the smooth and youthful body need enter. The female nude in particular has been subject to the double standard that considers naked bodies acceptable in classical art but objectionable or pornographic when grounded in the 'real' bodies of women. The reasons for the under-representation of the ageing body are manifold. In a society that associates beauty and power with youth, it is hardly surprising that the older woman remains culturally invisible. We are surrounded by images of the body that is to be looked at, not lived in. But where does the cut-off point occur between being seen and unseen? And who decides the age of ageing?

In their series of works entitled *Outrageous Agers* (2000), Rosy Martin and Kay Goodridge enter into and subvert conventional stereotypes of the older woman, using irony, parody and transgression to challenge the cultural invisibility of the ageing female body. Both humorous and serious in its message, their work questions the stigma of growing old, which so often becomes a process of de-eroticisation under the gaze of contemporary society. Furthermore, by engaging with the dynamics of representing the old(er) female nude, the absence of the older woman in visual art is challenged. The image leads the audience to question what it might mean to 'act your age'. Significantly, Martin and Goodridge turn the camera on themselves rather than photographing 'other' aged bodies.

In her work on the aesthetics of women and ageing, Joanna Frueh offers an interesting perspective on the perception of the older woman in contemporary society: 'The old(er) woman is doubly different, doubly degraded, and doubly injured by exterior identity: she is visibly female, different from men, and visibly aging, even when cosmetically altered, different from the young.'[1]

Desexualised, sagging, undesirable and troublesome, the body of the old(er) woman remains largely unseen and neglected by popular culture. Frueh goes on to describe how the older female body can be perceived as monstrous in its visible shapeshifting and undoing of feminine perfection. Her response to this is to propose what might be termed a 'monstrous erotics' of the ageing female nude based on experience and self-love, rather than fear and shame: 'The experienced body is deeply erotic, for it wears the lusts and (ab)uses of living... Perhaps the aged and aging female body can become an object of love, for the old(er) woman herself to have and to hold.'[2] In *Outrageous Agers*, the ageing woman is active, malleable, shifting and flexible; indeed, functional in every respect. The role of photography is shown to be central in developing an aesthetics of ageing and, by using a variety of techniques and sources, Martin and Goodridge confront the ageing issue head-on.

In a series of photographs shot in the changing rooms of the high-street store Top Shop, Martin and Goodridge engage with and perform the stereotype of 'mutton dressed as lamb' by trying on a range of trendy clubwear in sequins, leopardskin print and PVC. The combination of bare flesh and stretched fabric creates a sense of discomfort and unease as they force their bodies to fit

From the *Outrageous Agers* series 2000
© Rosy Martin and Kay Goodridge
Originals in colour – lightbox, duratrans

angles, which tend to focus equally on the textures, colours and movement of the fabric and the fragmented body of the model. The function of the changing-room mirror is also significant, with its associations of scrutiny, vanity and beauty as well as its more traditional link with self-portraiture. The mirror serves two other important functions: to reinforce the act of looking, both on behalf of the viewer as voyeur inside the changing room, and the artist as (fashion) model and photographer, and to highlight the performative nature of the images, that is, the trying on of youth.

The Top Shop images become more highly charged when viewed in relation to the frieze of bodyscapes. Interestingly, the artists' 'real' bodies are presented as a continuum in contrast to the fragmented snapshots inside the changing room. The difference between these gorgeous bodyscapes and the bodies squeezed uncomfortably into inappropriate clothes is startling. The use of double exposures highlights the notion of *becoming* an old(er) woman, as the body continually shifts and undergoes a series of changes and modifications, for example grey hair, wrinkles, etc. Here we see layers of skin and body parts—bellies, chins, hair, eyes — merging into each other to create a sense of the 'unstable, ever changing body'.[3] The act of looking at the undulating folds and contours of the skin becomes pleasurable and manifold, as though the artists are playfully interrogating our assumptions of how the ageing female body *should* appear. By juxtaposing a visual exploration of how it feels and looks to inhabit an ageing body with a sense of liberation corporeal, aesthetic and political, the absence of the older woman in visual art is profoundly challenged. Within a patriarchal frame, only the smooth, healthy body is considered an appropriate body type for art: anything 'other' is out of bounds/monstrous.

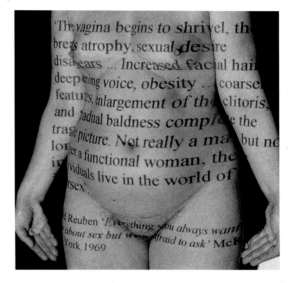

'The vagina begins to shrivel...'
From the *Outrageous Agers* series 2000
© Rosy Martin and Kay Goodridge

within fashion's parameters. Ironically, this is anything but a changing room — the true contours of the body can never fully be disguised by clothes. But there is also a sense of carnivalesque fun which derives from the ambiguity of the images as well as the telling gestural acts: in one shot we see bum and thighs squeezed into a pair of harsh-looking black PVC trousers and boob tube, and in another, the revealing plunge of a lycra dress is complimented by tendrils of hair, thus fitting an altogether more conventional fashion frame.

The montage-style images, mounted as light-boxes, parody current fashion photography's techniques and

In a series of scripto-visual works, an interesting conjunction between theory and practice takes place as Martin and Goodridge project theoretical texts on to their bodies. The fact that not all of the text is visible is conceptually significant: the distortion of the text mirrors the disruptive and excessive body that is pictured before us. The confrontation between real flesh and a text such as David Reuben's diatribe on the rapid decline of the older woman is a particularly challenging image, as the body effectively swallows the words whole:

'The vagina begins to shrivel, the breasts atrophy, sexual desire disappears... Increased facial hair, deepening voice, obesity... coarsened features, enlargement of the clitoris, and gradual baldness complete the tragic picture. Not really a man but no longer a functional woman, these individuals live in the world of intersex.'[4]

The authority of such normative and clinical statements is undermined by the presence of a body that is both dynamic and demanding: flesh overpowers word. The artists have also been careful to select affirmative texts to balance the more reductive excerpts, and use them in intriguing ways; for example, a paragraph from Luce Irigaray's *This Sex Which is Not One* is cleverly projected in such a way that the word 'play' is caught in the mirror thereby raising issues of mimesis, visibility and reflection.

There seems to be an affinity between photography and representing the ageing body which stems from the mutual associations between mirroring and reality. Women photographers such as Anne Noggle, Jacqueline Hayden and Melanie Manchot explore the aesthetics of ageing in very different ways. Significantly, Martin and Goodridge, like Noggle, turn the camera on themselves rather than photographing 'other' aged bodies. As viewers and inhabitants of ageing bodies, their practice establishes an intimate connection between the subject and the process of self-representation. This heightened sense of engagement with the embodied subject must surely be crucial in any attempt at re-framing the old(er) woman in visual art.

Jenny Saville's photographic self-portraits celebrate excessive flesh and sensuality, whilst confronting contemporary obsession with the thin and nubile youthful body. Just as Martin and Goodridge explore the all-consuming corporeality of the ageing female body, so too Saville plays with notions of monstrous otherness in breaking down the boundaries between the proper and improper body. Like the female monster in the horror film, Saville's bodies reach out to get you, to pull you in and, ultimately, destroy the boundaries between observed and observer. The malleability of the flesh is exploited with

profound effect in her self-portraits, where the surface of the image becomes pliable and dynamic. The process of monstering herself, of pushing her own flesh to the limits, renders the body in a perpetual state of flux which evokes a kind of 'monster/beauty', as termed by Frueh. This is perhaps one of the most interesting aspects of her work; it is her *own* body that she is referencing as culturally unacceptable. She is involved in a process of monstering *herself* rather than being monstered by society.

The collaborative *Closed Contact* series (1995-6) shows Saville's body in continual process, simultaneously recognisable and unrecognisable, and framed by the lens of the fashion photographer Glen Luchford. However, he is the collaborator, providing an ironic nuance. While the male fashion photographer in total control of the nude female model is the perfect trope of the phallocentric gaze, it is not Luchford, but Jenny Saville who is in control. She manipulates the gaze of the camera and she directs the frame. The immense scale of the photographs threatens to overwhelm us, creating a sense of awe and directness. Whereas the fixity of the traditional self-portrait confirms our relationship as spectator of the image, the sheer corporeal chaos depicted here breaks down that boundary and enables a different kind of viewing to take place.

It is useful to think about our own role as viewers of self-portraits and how we can play a key role in both making and engaging with the photographic image. Recent feminist film theory offers some fascinating ideas about how vision can become a process of embodiment and intercorporeality which seems relevant to Saville's work. Laura Marks, building on the theories of Gilles Deleuze, posits that 'The ideal relationship between viewer and image in haptic visuality is one of mutuality, in

which the viewer is more likely to lose herself, to lose her sense of proportion.'[5] Saville's proximity to the surface of the photograph challenges our sense of proportion and scale, and confuses the relationship between viewer and subject. Her body is squashed against the glass/frame so that our eyes can almost touch it — in other words, as Marks suggests, our vision becomes tactile.

In her analysis of the seven 'faces' of woman in the horror film, Barbara Creed locates the monstrous-feminine within the female reproductive body, which signifies transgressive femininity at its most dangerous and dynamic.[6] Saville's evocation of the monstrous-feminine in these photographs is active, threatening, transgressive and continually shifting. Her self-portraits demand an active response as excessive flesh threatens to envelop the viewer. Her primary subject is the female body and what it feels like to be an obese woman in a culture that defines the thin, nubile body as perfect. The monstrosity of these images does not derive from the fact that these are oversized women; rather, it is from the sheer scale of the paintings and photographs, the proximity of flesh to frame, and the fact that these bodies are often based on composites; a mingling of bodies and body parts.

The spread of flesh threatens to exceed the limits of the frame and yet somehow it remains contained within those margins. She portrays the *wholeness* and *fleshiness* of the female body, identifying it with defiance and dominance in direct contrast to traditional representations of the female nude as a beautiful, passive and idealised object. In Saville's work, the rolls and bulges of the female body become a source of magnificent and intense physicality. Here, visual pleasure is derived from seeing realistic flesh, with all its bumps and veins, and not airbrushed perfection. Saville's images react against media stereotypes of the female body by depicting a body which is flabby, veined and drooping, not glamourised and surgically enhanced like so many cultural constructions of femininity.

In returning to Marks' notion of haptic visuality, that is, the powerful metaphor of the eye touching the skin of the film, an embodied mode of viewing can be a pleasurable and sensual act. Isabella Ramsay's work invites such a response. Her images of the female body as landscape seduce the eye into tracing the curves and folds of flesh until we become lost, enveloped. As Marks states: '...haptic visuality does imply a critique of mastery, the mastery implicit in optical visuality, but it is through a desiring and often pleasurable relationship to the image that this critique is bodied forth.'[7]

Making her own body the subject of her work was an important step for Ramsay in reinstating her own identity as a woman, both on a personal and political level, as well as marking the physical changes associated with the ageing female body: 'I felt that something was missing. As my body became more used, in terms of childbirth, operations, scars, breaks, change of size, texture, colour and age, I became aware that I was not, in the main, represented in history, politically or artistically, nor in the media, or on the corporate ladder.'[8] In her series *Topographies of the Body* (1999), Ramsay represents her own naked body, as well as the bodies of others, as landscape on a grand scale. These large format photographs command our attention, confusing the boundaries between inside and outside, surface and flesh. The inclusion of narrative texts alongside the photographs emphasises the individuality of her models and offers another perspective on what it means to represent the nude in contemporary society.

Topographies of the Body; 'other' ways of looking, 1999
© Isabella Ramsay
2m x 1.5m

The pleasure in viewing these images stems from the process of bodily mapping: the contours of the bodies represented materialise female desire and sensuality. Ramsay wants us to engage actively with this materialisation, to read the texts that accompany the images, offering a fruitful and meaningful interaction. Like those of Saville, these images lead us back to Frueh's notion of monster/beauty, forming the basis of her re-conception of the erotic: 'Monster/beauty eroticises the midlife female body, develops love between women, embraces without degrading or aggrandizing bodies that differ from one's own in age, race, sex and shape.'[9] What Frueh and Ramsay both convey is the pleasure in the 'non-ideal' body, a body that is inscribed by experience, knowledge and sexuality.

Alexa Wright's work is focused on the issue of difference. In a culture that values the parts of the body over the whole, what happens to the body with missing or deformed limbs? How does society, in effect, monster these bodies? Margrit Shildrick defines the monstrous

thus: 'Above all, it is the corporeal ambiguity and fluidity, the troublesome lack of fixed definition, the refusal to be either one thing or the other, that marks the monstrous as a site of disruption.'[10] Rendering the disabled body visible in a society that values the healthy, whole body is a challenge facing many contemporary artists. In Wright's recent work, the breaking of corporeal boundaries, and the ensuing fear that this may arouse, is central. The primary focus here is the boundary between self and body and the extent to which this may be challenged by 'othered' bodies, such as amputees and transplant patients.

Collaboration is a central aspect of Wright's work. In the *After Image* series (1997), Wright explores the metaphor of the cyborg in relation to prosthetics. The project involved a collaboration with a neurologist and a neuropsychologist in order to research the phenomenon of phantom limbs, whereby amputees retain a sense of their absent body part for years after their operation. The main thrust of the project was to visualise these absent limbs, using the genre of portraiture as a normalising context. Each image aims to give flesh to the missing body part by using digital manipulation; in this case, the real arm that existed prior to the prosthetic arm. Wright questions our readiness to identify different bodies as abnormal or monstrous by placing the individual within their own space, their normal everyday surroundings. Her work also leads to questions of authenticity; what is the 'real' body? Is it the one we experience or the one we see? How can new technologies help us see further into the body?

Wright's series 'I' (1998-9) questions the authenticity of the body and how we come to know what is 'normal' in Western society. She creates disruptive images that challenge our attitudes towards physical disability,

From the series 'I' (1) 1998-9
© Alexa Wright
Digital print, 30" x 40"

proposes), in terms of knowing, in the phenomenological sense, as opposed to seeing the body, is of primary importance here.[11]

In a challenging image of the female nude, Wright maps her facial features and lower body on to the upper body of Sonia Barnes. The act of representing the disabled body within the framework of the female nude presents a direct challenge to aesthetic boundaries. The baroque setting plays a key function in deconstructing fixed notions of disabled bodies. None of the usual signs inscribed upon the disabled body, such as a wheelchair, are present. The elegance of the purple chaise longue is a strategic replacement that helps define the sitter as a person rather than an object. The artist's use of digital manipulation adds a further layer of meaning; curiously, the sitter began to identify with the body imaged, as though the legs and feet belonged to her. In this way, the photograph erases the notion of an 'other' body and replaces it with an alternative sense of wholeness that only the subject can experience.

In an interesting play on the Venus de Milo theme, Wright creates a striking image of a woman who oozes confidence and glamour. The interplay between bodies is particularly important — the head and one arm of the statue remain outside the frame. The reflection in the window hovers between the human figure and the statue to create a shifting sense of wholeness and fragmentation. Significantly, the reflected figure has its back turned, the act of looking away from that which we find confrontational. Like Sonia Barnes, the sitter in this case Catherine Long, felt able to identify with the image as her own body. Commenting on the photograph, she says: 'At first I felt my shoulder looked wrong on someone else's body, but now I don't. Now I see it as me.'[12] This statement

After Image RD2 1997
© Alexa Wright
22" x 30"

has far-reaching implications for the notion of knowing virtual bodies — the fact that the sitter, on viewing the image, felt that her shoulder belonged to another body is profound.

These images represent troublesome corporeality, not because of the disability represented but because of our fixed notions of beauty and normality. While Wright's earlier images have close links with the monstrous in terms of the threat posed by viewing the abject interior of the body, the 'I' series raises ethical issues about the way the female body is monstered in contemporary society. These images open up new modes of knowing and experiencing

beauty and the female body. Each image features a rich baroque backdrop, and all but one show the artist's facial features mapped on to the bodies of women with a disability. These images raise important issues concerning beauty, ugliness, fear and exclusion, as well as highlighting the relationship between the body and the self-utilising new technologies. While Wright herself is non-disabled, she overcomes this potentially problematic position by engaging in an active dialogue with her sitters, as opposed to simply looking at them as different bodies. Indeed, the collaborative aspect of the project is paramount; to experience the body (as Elizabeth Grosz

the body by emphasising the collaborative aspect of the work. These women are involved in a process of merging and transforming their own bodies, using the techniques of photo-imaging, thus defying the corporeal limits of material flesh. In doing so, our readiness to label atypical bodies is challenged.

The importance of collaboration is also emphasised in *Skin* (2000) where people with severe skin conditions, such as vitiligo and psoriasis, describe their experiences in a series of texts displayed alongside photographs of affected fragments of their skin. Wright juxtaposes the surface of the skin with richly patterned and decorative fabrics which compel us to look; we are seduced by the beauty of the fabric, the stunning colours and the rich materiality, and yet the accompanying texts pull us back by reminding us of the reality of living with a disabling skin condition. The importance of the text/image interplay is clearly evident in this series in the sense that reading the accompanying texts renders the fragments of bodies whole again. Wright succeeds in negotiating the potential difficulties of dealing with difference by developing an intimate knowledge of her subject matter. She forms relationships with collaborators that balance the ethical and aesthetic concerns inherent in her work.

One of the most interesting aspects of the work discussed here is the artists' interdisciplinary and collaborative approach to their practice. Martin and Goodridge work together to create challenging self-portraits and draw on a wide range of visual and textual references. Saville collaborates with a fashion photographer in probing the limits of her own body, while both Ramsay and Wright forge particular and specific relationships with their models. Wright has also collaborated with numerous practitioners and researchers

from other disciplines in what has become 'ongoing process-based exploratory work'.[13] This has important resonances for women's art practice as a whole, particularly in relation to the use of innovative technologies in creating new forms of portraiture. Our understanding of the self-portrait is further enhanced by the strategic interplay between text and image. The texture of talk, as Marks observes, serves as a counterpart to the image which activates the senses and enables a more intimate viewing to take place. The works discussed here challenge how we view images of ourselves and others, and it is our relationship with those others that is fundamental to our understanding of difference and, therefore, to a re-negotiation of the culturally determined boundaries surrounding the body and self-portraiture.

ENDNOTES

1   Frueh, Joanna, 'Visible Difference: Women Artists and Aging', in M. Pearsall (ed.), *The Other Within Us: Feminist Explorations of Women and Aging* (Colorado: Westview Press, 1997), p. 202.

2   Frueh, 'Visible Difference', p. 212.

3   '*Outrageous Agers*: A Collaboration Between Rosy Martin and Kay Goodridge' (press release) (Wolverhampton: Light House, 2000).

4   Reuben, David, *Everything You Always Wanted to Know About Sex, But Were Afraid to Ask* (New York: McKay, 1969).

5   Marks, Laura, *The Skin of the Film: Intercultural Cinema, Embodiment, and the Senses* (Durham: Duke University Press, 2000), p. 184.

6   Creed, Barbara, *The Monstrous Feminine: Film, Feminism and Psychoanalysis* (London: Routledge, 1993).

7   Marks, *Skin of the Film*, p. 184.

8   Ramsay, Isabella, 'Topographies of the Body' (exhibition talk, 1999).

9   Frueh, Joanna, *Monster/Beauty* (Berkeley: California University Press, 2001), p. 11.

10   Shildrick, Margrit, 'This Body Which Is Not One: Dealing with Differences', in Featherstone, Mike (ed.), *Body Modification* (London: Sage Publications, 2000), pp. 77-92 (p. 78).

11   Grosz, Elizabeth, *Space, Time and Perversion* (London: Routledge, 1995).

12   Wright, Alexa, '*I*', exhibition leaflet (Edinburgh: Napier University, 1999).

13   Ride, Peter, Foreword to *Alexa Wright: Intimate Strangers/recent works* (London: CARTE, 2003).

ZINEB SEDIRA

from the series Self Portrait

The photographic series *Self Portraits* represents Algerian women and myself dressed in a Haïk, the Algerian veil. Here, through the titles and imageries, I am drawing references to the Christian and Muslim tradition of veiling. The veil, the triptych format, and the Arab body destabilise and disrupt signs, throwing into question markers of ethnic and cultural difference by evoking icons and symbols that link cultures rather than separate them. Furthermore, *Self Portraits* was born in response to the way the Muslim veil is too often exposed in western media as fixed and monolithic — a homogeneous, uniform, black veil.

Self Portrait or The Trinity 2000 (tryptic)
Self Portrait or The Virgin Mary 2000 (dyptic)

TRISH MORRISSEY

WWM

Laura
Kate
Karen
Lisa
Tanya
Indigo

Courage in the Face of History:
Cross-Cultural Portraits

Sandra Matthews

A portrait is always more than a representation of an individual human being. Like people themselves, portraits store multiple narratives within, offering only enigmatic hints to onlookers. A portrait can be the starting point for unravelling the narratives of history and culture so central to each person's life.[1] Four American women artists — Alma Lopez, Delilah Montoya, Sheila Pinkel and Meridel Rubenstein — use photographic portraits to dramatise powerful narratives of history and culture. Although these artists have not been influenced by each other, their work is connected by a complex web of ideas. All four work with histories of war and upheaval, struggle and resistance; all employ myths to tell their stories; and all present models of courage. Though they work with culturally specific material — Lopez and Montoya with the Chicano icon of the Virgin of Guadalupe, and Pinkel and Rubenstein with postwar portraits of Cambodians and Vietnamese — all four artists deal with issues of physical, cultural, and spiritual survival that transcend the specifics of culture.

Although a military conflict may officially end when the fighting stops, wars have consequences that reverberate for many generations. At the end of the Mexican-American war, in 1848, thousands of Mexicans living in northern Mexico suddenly became, by treaty, Mexican-Americans. More than 150 years later, Chicanos — present day Mexican-Americans — still frequently suffer discrimination in US society. The Virgin of Guadalupe is a potent icon used by Mexicans and Chicanos as a sign of cultural identity and a source of support in times of difficulty.

The story of the Virgin of Guadalupe's apparition is important to understanding her meaning. According to legend, the Virgin appeared several times to a humble Aztec (Nahuatl) Indian named Juan Diego in 1531, ten years after the Spanish conquest of Mexico. Juan Diego had recently converted to Catholicism. She appeared to him on the hill at Tepeyac, the former site of the temple to the Aztec mother goddess Tonantzin. The Virgin commanded Juan Diego to tell the local bishop he must build a church to her on this site. When the bishop asked for proof of her appearance, the Virgin instructed Juan Diego to gather flowers from a nearby location. Juan Diego found roses blooming there, although it was winter, and he filled his cape (tilma) with them to bring to the bishop. When he opened his cape in the presence of the bishop, the roses spilled out and both men saw that an image of the Virgin had been miraculously imprinted on the inside of the 'tilma'. This cloth image still resides in the Basilica of Our Lady of Guadalupe, which was in fact built on the hill at Tepeyac, on the outskirts of present-day Mexico City.

In this way the Virgin of Guadalupe, with her church on the temple site of an equivalent Aztec goddess, provided a way for the conquered Indians to outwardly practise Catholicism and still be connected to their own culture, to take 'a subversive path away from the patriarchal, Jesus-centered European church toward an Indian, matriarchal spirituality'.[2] The Guadalupe appears in countless paintings as a dark-skinned Madonna standing on a crescent moon which is supported from below by a small angel. She wears a cloak decorated with stars, and her body is surrounded with 'rayas', rays of the sun. She is a hybrid figure who graciously mixes conquest with resistance. While many Mexicans revere her, calling her the mother of their people, she has taken on another level of meaning in Chicano culture, as a symbol of minority pride. When farm workers in California, under the leadership of Cesar Chavez, successfully struck for fair treatment, her image was on their banners. Thus she is called on to support the status quo by making it bearable, and also called on to support the struggle for revolutionary change.

Delilah Montoya takes the icon of the Guadalupe back to its Indian roots. She has focused specifically on the tattoos of the Virgin frequently found on the backs and arms of Chicano men. Montoya knows that certain Aztec rituals prescribe the skinning of a female sacrificial victim, whose skin is then worn ceremonially by a male who will also be sacrificed. She therefore feels that skin is a particularly appropriate 'canvas' for the image of the Guadalupe. The tattooed image becomes like a 'second skin', worn on a man's back as a protection from unseen harm.[3]

Montoya also explores the gender-specific meanings of the Guadalupe. Apparently human skins were worn in Aztec ritual to bring the powers of male and female energies together. Her monumental work *El Guadalupano*

El Guadalupano, 1998
© Delilah Montoya
9.5' x 15'

ethnicity. It is thought that he was jailed not for a crime he had committed but as a possible informant on members of a gang with which he had formerly been involved.[4]

In a tragic twist, shortly after posing for this picture, Felix Martinez was murdered in prison, leaving behind his wife and young daughter. When exhibiting this mural, Montoya makes it into an altar with candles and offerings laid out beneath it. Her original intention was to recreate a shrine to the Virgin of Guadalupe, but the installation has also turned into a memorial for Felix. He has become a martyred figure, who was caught between the demands of two masculine cultures — the gang culture of the barrio and a flawed criminal justice system. His tattoo represents an attempt to express cultural identity and personhood against all odds, and poignantly invokes the needed qualities of maternal protection. In his body he brings together, without resolution, the extreme polarities of 'macho' masculinity and nurturing femininity.

While Montoya looks at the Guadalupe image in relation to men, Alma Lopez addresses the possible meanings of the Guadalupe for women. Her digital composition entitled *Our Lady* allows the Virgin to come down from her pedestal and relate more directly to the viewer, as a strong, beautiful Chicana woman who owns her own body and is not ashamed to show it. Lopez was inspired by an essay by Sandra Cisneros, which speaks of the traditional Guadalupe as 'an ideal so lofty and unrealistic' that it is difficult for real women to identify with her.[5] Usually the Guadalupe's body, including her feet, is completely covered in cloth. This Guadalupe is clothed only with an open cloak and multicolored roses, which modestly cover her breasts and genitals. Lopez has recast the traditional iconography of the Virgin, taking the design on her cape from an Aztec stone carving of the dismembered body of the goddess

Our Lady, 1999
© Alma Lopez
Giclee/Iris Print on Canvas
17.5" x 14"
(special thanks to Raquel Salinas and Raquel Gutierrez)

Coyolxauhqui.[6] The angel supporting the crescent moon has become a nude woman with large maternal breasts and wings of the Viceroy butterfly.[7] But, most importantly, Lopez's model, Raquel Salinas, projects an image of female power. She becomes a positive role-model, standing up for her gender as well as her culture, courageously providing an alternative to the all-nurturing, ever-supportive Virgin. This Virgin asserts herself under difficult circumstances.

In fact the image was a risky one to make. Lopez's version of the Guadalupe, distinctly feminine but not particularly maternal, immediately stirred up vocal controversy among the most serious of the Virgin's

is a mural-sized composite photograph picturing, larger than life, the head and upper body of a male prisoner, posing with his hands handcuffed behind him. He is wearing prison-issue clothing, the upper garment dropped to reveal a large tattoo of the Virgin of Guadalupe on his muscular back. Montoya's image is a portrait both of the man, taken from behind, and of the image of the Virgin, facing the viewer. This double-gendered image is full of irony: the icon of the Virgin is a sign of Chicano cultural pride, yet this man, Felix Martinez, has lost his autonomy by being imprisoned, perhaps in part because of his

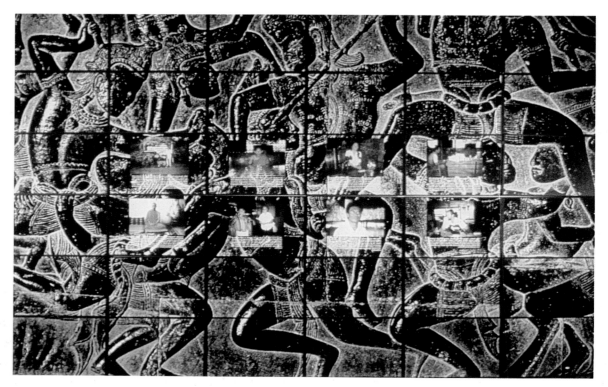

Remember Cambodia: Survivors, 1997
© Sheila Pinkel
66" x 102"

Sheila Pinkel and Meridel Rubenstein are also interested in building bridges between cultures. Their work comes in the aftermath of the wars in Vietnam and Cambodia in the 1960s and early 1970s. As young North Americans, Pinkel and Rubenstein both actively protested against the US military involvement in these countries. Both independently have returned to south-east Asia years later, to investigate the continuing impact of those wars. They also have each, as adults, become deeply interested in Buddhist meditation.

Driven by the desire to know about the long-term impact of war in south-east Asia, for which the US had heavy responsibility, Sheila Pinkel made a series of extended trips in the 1990s to Cambodian and Hmong refugee camps in Thailand, and to Cambodia, Vietnam and Laos, where she gathered photographs and stories of survivors of the war. She has also followed closely the lives of several Hmong and Cambodian refugee families in the US. Based on these experiences, Pinkel has produced a large multifaceted work entitled *Indochina Document*, which she continues to expand and update. The images reproduced here come from the portion of this work entitled *Remember Cambodia*. They are structured as large-scale grids, the rectangles of each grid together forming a large black and white background image. The background images represent details from the stone carvings found in the ancient Cambodian temple of Angkor Wat. These carvings picture the epic stories of classical Hinduism, the precursor to Cambodia's present-day Buddhist culture. Pinkel has inserted color photographs and text elements into the grids. In this way, her portraits of present-day individuals are seen against a backdrop of mythic proportions.

In the first grid, Pinkel pays homage to people she met who acted, often in the midst of genocide and personal

devotees. Their principal objection centred around the portrayal of this sacred mother-figure as a real woman with a real body.[8] Although those offended by Lopez's image are a tiny minority, the intensity of their response is a reminder of how powerful a force an icon can be. Yet surely the icon can also be a force for change, as it has been in the past, responsive to shifting cultural needs. In the long Mexican tradition of establishing a personal relationship with the Virgin, Lopez has created an image that speaks to her personal concern for the needs of contemporary women.

Both Lopez and Montoya honour an important cultural and religious icon, while at the same time they work to de-mythologise it, to show where the myth does not apply. They connect the Virgin of Guadalupe with contemporary political issues, reminding us that this icon served political purposes from the start. Since Chicano culture is a hybrid culture, formed out of the experience of displacement, these images are already internally multicultural. But in addition to contributing to the ongoing vitality of Chicano culture, Lopez and Montoya are also building bridges between their cultural tradition and the rest of the world.

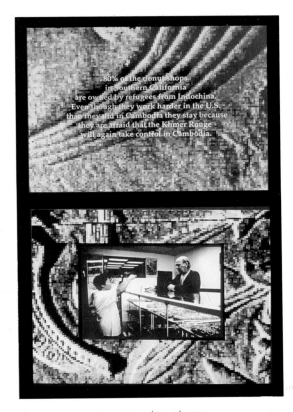

Donut Shop (detail) 1996
© Sheila Pinkel
11" x 18"

Forest (detail) 2000-1
© Meridel Rubenstein

trauma, to preserve human and cultural life. Eight remarkable individuals — five Cambodians and three Westerners — are pictured, with their stories briefly recounted beneath their portraits (see Appendix A). Their achievements include translating key Buddhist texts into Khmer and distributing the texts to temples throughout Cambodia, reuniting hundreds of refugee children with their families, establishing a psychiatric centre in a large refugee camp, advocating women's rights, and instructing a generation who had lost the opportunity for education in

Buddhist practice and tradition. Because the devastation of the war made many Cambodians strangers to their own traditions, cultural repair was accomplished by both outsiders and insiders. These individuals attended to the physical, emotional and spiritual needs of a traumatised people, often at significant cost to themselves. The background image against which we see them is a carving of an epic battle, the Battle of Kuruksetva. In front of this ancient image of figures in heated combat, Pinkel has placed the small, bright pictures of these people who effectively countered the effects of massive destruction. They are quiet war heroes of a very special kind, significantly different from the heroes of battle pictured behind them.

In the second grid, Pinkel has concentrated on a specific family of Cambodian refugees living in Los Angeles. The small inserted words and images describe their struggle to survive. One text insert reads: 'For the last eight years they have been working eighteen hours a day, seven days a week, making and selling donuts. They have supported a large extended family in the US and continue to send money to relatives in Cambodia. Every night he wears a shirt with the image of Angkor Wat. He thinks he can last another five years. She laughs and says that she is "tired, so tired".' Pinkel places images of the family members at work in their doughnut shop against a huge image of a stone carving representing the giant demon Ravana 'using all his strength to shift Mount Kailasa, the Himalayan abode of the god Siva, back into position after an accident tipped it to one side'. Pinkel sees this hard-working family as engaged in a similar struggle, trying to set their lives back into proper position after terrible personal and cultural upheaval. That the man wears a shirt with the image of Angkor Wat is a moving

detail which seems to speak of the power of images to perpetuate culture across time and space, as well as of his attempt to remain culturally 'grounded' as he occupies a space somewhere between Cambodia and the US, not yet comfortable in a hybrid identity.

In both works the carved stone image in the background contextualises the present-day individuals, and lends their struggles epic status. By visually connecting the recent traumatic events and immigrant struggles of Cambodians to the nation's rich artistic and religious history, Pinkel demonstrates the possibility of continuity in the face of cataclysm. Her work participates in the simultaneous cultural reclamation and adaptation that preoccupies Cambodians today. As such it also speaks to issues faced by diaspora communities and threatened cultures everywhere.

While Pinkel's extensive journeys involved the in-depth gathering of a 'peoples' history' of the war and its aftermath in Cambodia, Meridel Rubenstein's journey was part of a different, poetic project. The two works shown here are from an exhibition entitled *Trees at Sea*, one part of an ambitious multi-media project that is still underway and which Rubenstein calls *Joan's Arc: Vietnam*. In the exhibition *Trees at Sea*, Rubenstein first draws a parallel between centuries-old trees and human survivors of war. Thus the image entitled *Forest* pictures the abbot, abbess, novice and nuns of the Tu Hieu and Dieu Ngheim Pagodas in Vietnam, representing them as firmly rooted individuals together constituting a human forest. Yet this translucent group portrait is laminated between two pieces of glass, and the glass then stands upright in a small wooden dugout canoe — a boat made from the trunk of a tree ('a tree at sea'). So the forest is both rooted and mobile, potentially or actually journeying. And in fact these monks and nuns are part of the monastery from which the influential monk, Thich Nhat Hanh, journeyed out to plant the seeds of Buddhist thought abroad. Sandblasted on to the fragile but luminous glass is a delicate additional image of the veins of the leaves of a Bodhi tree, the kind of tree under which the Buddha was sitting when he first attained enlightenment. Rubenstein is interested in the coexistence of contradictory elements such as power and fragility, rootedness and mobility, tradition and transformation.

This piece is accompanied by a sister work entitled *Volunteers*, which is also constructed as a group portrait sandwiched between pieces of glass, standing in a wooden dugout canoe. 'Volunteer' is a gardener's term referring to a plant that grows in an unexpected place. Eight 'volunteers' stand looking out at the viewer, overlaid with a sandblasted image of wooden boat-hulls. They are male and female, all ages and races, each holding an object of personal value small enough to be taken on a journey. Five

Volunteers, 2000–1
© Meridel Rubenstein
Gallery installation view
13.7" x 48" dye-transfer film laminated between glass
in nineteenth-century dugout 70" x 14" x 10"

of them are Vietnamese-born individuals who were adopted into US families. Two others are a US Vietnam veteran and his Vietnamese wife, the child of Viet Cong parents. The last is Mr Mai Van On, who, although he was fighting on the other side, saved the man who is now US Senator John McCain from drowning when his plane was shot down into a Vietnamese lake. According to the story, which takes on a mythic quality although it is true, he then saved him a second time when his fellow soldiers wanted to shoot him, saying "You can't shoot, I saved him." All of these people have made human alliances across battle lines, have touched the enemy.

For Rubenstein, the ability of people to redefine terms such as 'enemy' represents courage. Her subjects are heroic in their ability to survive, adapt, and cross boundaries. Her metaphors are from nature rather than history. Her interest is less in the specific facts of the Vietnam War than in its mythic dimensions as a disaster that uprooted individuals, forcing them to journey and regenerate.

While much cross-cultural photographic work presents

an exotic spectacle to the curious viewer, neither Pinkel's nor Rubenstein's work invites this kind of voyeurism. Their attempts to bridge cultural boundaries are made in a spirit of reconciliation and human connection. If the people who figure in their work are held up as inspiring examples, they are also represented as humble individuals, characters in larger stories. Both artists portray specific people as the unknowing heroes of myths — myths of passage, of rescue and survival, of heroism and sacrifice. Yet the actual portraits are all the more moving because of their modesty. These heroes do not strike 'heroic' poses, but appear in their everyday guises.

Lopez and Montoya have 'de-mythologised' the Virgin of Guadalupe, making her meaningful in new ways both within and beyond Chicano culture. Pinkel and Rubenstein have, on the other hand, 'mythologised' a group of actual individuals, also articulating their stories for a broader audience. Taken together, the works of all four artists remind us that culture is never static or singular, and that bridging between cultures is a creative act that can take many forms. These works bear important messages about the possibilities for sustaining cultural continuity and also for implementing positive cultural change, if we have the courage.

ENDNOTES

1   I use the word 'culture' here to refer to the customs and beliefs defining a group of people, which in turn shape and are shaped by the experiences of race, class and gender.

2   Martinez, Ruben, 'The Undocumented Virgin', in Ana Castillo (ed.), *Goddess of the Americas: La Diosa de las Americas* (New York: Riverhead Books, 1996), p. 101.

3   Montoya's recent work includes images of male and female bodies tattooed with the Guadalupe. Using digital technology, she creates the illusion that their skins have been 'peeled' off and exist as free-floating objects.

4   For a full account of Felix Martinez's story, see Montoya's article entitled 'On Photographic Digital Imaging', in *Aztlan* 27, 1, Spring 2002.

5   Cisneros, Sandra, 'Guadalupe the Sex Goddess,' in *Goddess of the Americas*, p. 48.

6   According to legend (recounted in Cherrie Moraga's essay 'El Mito Azteca' in *Goddess of the Americas*), when Coyolxauhqui learns that her mother is about to give birth to Huitzilopochtli, the god of war, she conspires with her siblings to kill her mother. However, Huitzilopochtli is forewarned and, at the moment of birth, he kills and dismembers Coyolxauhqui. Lopez informed me that the carving of her dismembered body was placed by the Aztecs on the ground at the entrance to a temple, so that people would walk on it. By using this carving as the visual design on the cloak of *Our Lady*, she is reviving the memory of this daughter-goddess.

7   Lopez uses the Viceroy butterfly as a symbol: the Viceroy's wing patterns mimic those of the Monarch butterfly, which migrates annually back and forth across the US/Mexican border. The Viceroy benefits from this mimicry because the Monarch is poisonous to predators while it is not. Lopez uses this imagery to symbolise the actual vulnerability of Chicanos in the US.

8   For a detailed record of the controversy, including emails Lopez received both attacking and defending *Our Lady*, see her website at www.almalopez.net.

APPENDIX A

Text from 'Remember Cambodia: Survivors', by Sheila Pinkel.

Peter Gyalley Pap graduated from the University of Massachusetts with a PhD in theology. He did his dissertation on the history of Cambodian spiritual practice. From 1975-8 spiritual leaders, temples and texts were destroyed by the Khmer Rouge. Thus, young Buddhist novitiates at Site 2, a Cambodian refugee camp at the Thai/Cambodian border, had no books or elders to teach them about the history of Cambodian Buddhism. Peter showed them his dissertation video tapes and taught them about the practice. In this way he was able to fill a crucial gap in their knowledge, which allowed the next generation of monks at Site 2 to be educated.

Venerable Vinayathavo Phanoeum moved from temple to temple while fleeing from aerial bombing prior to 1975. He finally escaped to Thailand and spent ten years learning Thai and translating the original Buddhist Dharma by hand into Khmer. He emigrated to the United States in the mid-1980s and continued work on the book. In 1995 he published a printed version of the Dharma, which he took to Cambodia and distributed to temples throughout the country to rebuild spiritual practice, which had been weakened by the war.

Margot Grant went to Site 2 from Australia to help refugees get housing and healthcare. She helped them find protection from abduction, bombings and thieves. She made sure that hospital patients had adequate medical care and nutrition. Her son, Tim, started the Landmine Awareness Program at Site 2. Margot and Tim were captured, and subsequently released, by the Khmer Rouge when they ventured into Cambodia.

The Venerable Monychendo understood the important place which the temple has in the lives of village people in Cambodia. He was also concerned about the weakening of the memory of Buddhist practice because of the destruction of the spiritual community in Cambodia. He set up a school which gave young men training in Buddhist practice at Site 2. In 1992 he returned to Cambodia to set up a temple near an area controlled by the Khmer Rouge.

Mme Ung Yok Khoan was the president of the Khmer Women's Association at Site 2. From 1975-8 she worked as a farmer, pretending that she was illiterate so that she would not be killed. At Site 2 she encouraged women to get an education, take financial charge of their households and be more assertive with their husbands. She also started courses for women in human rights so that they would learn to honour themselves and one another. Her dream was to return to Cambodia and set up interconnected women's groups around the country which would facilitate women's self-determination.

Hong Setha was the son of two mathematics professors. From 1975-8 he worked in a child labour camp and, thus, was never able to finish high school. In 1979, he fled to Site 2 where he found his brother, his only surviving relative. He got married and had two children while in the camp. When he returned to Cambodia in 1992, he stayed with his father-in-law in the country. However, soldiers came to his house threatening to kill his family if they did not reveal the whereabouts of his brother. He immediately relocated his family to Phnom Penh.

Mme Man lived in Phnom Penh before 1975. From 1975-8 she was forced to work as a farmer. A Khmer Rouge soldier wanted to marry her daughter and when Mme Man protested that the girl was too young, several soldiers prepared to kill her. She finally allowed the marriage to save her own life. After the war, forced marriages were annulled. She and her family fled to Site 2. There, Mme Man established a psychiatric centre for traditional herbal and Western healing. Her daughter was a mute recluse living in this centre. The last time I saw her daughter she was being smuggled out of Site 2 to return to Phnom Penh to enter a nunnery.

Doug Hulcher, a teacher and photographer, realised that many Cambodian children became orphans when their families emigrated from the camps. From 1980-92 he devoted his life, without pay, to doing the paperwork and legal research which allowed Laotian and Cambodian refugee children to find their families abroad. During this period, due to his efforts, over 1,100 children were united with their families.

APPENDIX B

Meridel Rubenstein: Volunteers, 2000-1

My T. Pham, age 34, adopted to Minnesota family from Saigon for polio operations, father killed for helping her to escape.

Michael Dreyer, age 26, born Gia Dinh, S. Vietnam, adopted to Holland, Michigan, lives in Tempe, Arizona.

Heather Kim Degenhardt, age 28, born Saigon, adopted as infant to Maine, lives in NYC.

Sierra Barron, age 4, adopted to Phoenix, Arizona, from S. Vietnam.

Phuong Cunningham, married Danny late 1980s, from S. Vietnam near Camau and a Viet Cong family.

Khiem Van Hoang Royden Nagy, age 9, adopted Tariffeville, Connecticut, from Hue, Vietnam.

Danny Cunningham, US Vietnam Veteran, from Taos, NM, returned to Vietnam to live and marry.

Mr Mai Van On, Hanoi, the soldier who saved Senator John McCain from drowning in West lake in 1967, and then protected him from comrades' bullets.

Forest 2000-1

Abbot, Abbess, novice and nuns from Tu Hieu and Dieu Ngheim Pagodas, Hue City with bodhi leaf, the root monastery of peace activist, Thich Nhat Hanh

Biographical Notes

MARK DURDEN, born Stourbridge, West Midlands, England, 1964; studied Fine Art at Exeter College of Art and Glasgow School of Art, and the History and Theory of Art at the University of Kent (MA and PhD). He is an artist and writer, and is currently Reader in History and Theory of Photography at the University of Derby. He has published extensively on photography, contributing essays and articles to *Art Monthly*, *Creative Camera*, *Portfolio*, *Source*, *Afterimage* and *Parachute*. He co-edited the book *Face On: Photography as Social Exchange* (Black Dog Press, 2000), and contributed to the book on Dorothea Lange for the recent Phaidon 55 series. He has just published an essay for Paul Seawright's photographic book, *Hidden*, and is currently researching a book on photography theory.

BETH YARNELLE EDWARDS, born Johnstown, Pennsylvania, USA, 1950; taught English as a second language at college level before beginning to study photography in 1992, gaining a Master of Fine Arts in Photography from San Jose State University in 1998. Her work has been widely exhibited and collected in the United States and Europe. Numerous publications include: *European Photography*, *Photo Nouvelles*, *fotoMAGAZIN*, *The New Yorker*, *Harper's* and *The New York Times Magazine*. For the past six years, she has worked on her series *Suburban Dreams*, a visual exploration of people, places and things in middle-class California suburbs. She combines fine art practice with occasional editorial work, commissions and teaching.

CARYN FAURE WALKER, born Kew Gardens, New York, USA; is an American writer and curator based in London. Educated in art practice (sculpture), aesthetics and curatorship at New York University, St Martin's School of Art, The Royal College of Art and City University. She was co-founder of *Artscribe* (1975) and editor of *Make: the magazine of women's art* (1990-1). She has contributed to a variety of publications including *Art Monthly*, *Contemporary*, *The Museums Journal* and *Portfolio*. She is also a freelance curator who works with contemporary art, new media and site-based work. Key curated exhibitions and publications include: *The Green Room Project* (Bath/Southampton, England, 1995-7), *Sleuth; Investigations in Film Noir, Video, Photography and Electronic Media* (Barbican, London, 2000) and the exhibition and book *Magnetic North, Finnish Installation Photography of the 90s* (The New Art Gallery Walsall, 2001).

JANE FLETCHER, born Epsom, Surrey, England, 1967; is a Midlands-based writer. She has a PhD in Photography History and Theory, and is the co-editor of *I-Spy: Representations of Childhood* (I. B. Tauris, 2000). She has contributed articles and reviews to various magazines including *Afterimage*, *The Art Book*, *The British Journal of Photography*, *Portfolio* and *Source*.

RACHEL GEAR, born Huddersfield, Durham, England, 1972; studied English, History of Art and Psychology and Modern Literature: Theory and Practice at the University of Leicester (BA (Hons) and MA). She is currently writing up her PhD thesis at Loughborough University on the representation of the monstrous-feminine in the work of contemporary women artists. Published articles include 'Trying It On', *Make: the magazine of women's art* (April 2000), and 'Framing the Monstrous-Feminine: Issues and Practices', *Massage*, vol. 5 (October 1999), www.nomadnet.org/massage.html.

CATRIONA GRANT, born Dunfermline, Scotland, 1964; gained her BA (Hons) Fine Art from the Glasgow School of Art in 1986, and an MSc Electronic Imaging from Duncan of Jordanstone School of Art and Design, Dundee in 2001. She is an Edinburgh based artist working with lens-based and digital media to create work for exhibition and installation. She lectures at Edinburgh College of Art, and works with community groups on arts projects. She has been the recipient of a number of commissions and residencies including an EMARE Residency (2001), a hospital-based public art commission as part of the Fusion, Artlink Edinburgh project (2001) and a New Media Scotland Digital Art commission (2000). Publications include: *My Father is the Wise Man of the Village* (Fruitmarket Gallery, Edinburgh, 2002); *A Companion Guide to Photography in the National Galleries of Scotland* (National Galleries of Scotland, 2001); and *Blue Skies* (Stills Gallery, Edinburgh, 2001).

PAUL JOBLING, born Durham, England; studied History of Art and Philosophy at University College London and undertook postgraduate research at the Royal College of Art and the University of Warwick. He is currently Senior Lecturer in History of Art and Design at the University of Brighton, and has particular research interests in the intertextuality of word and image and issues of identity in advertising, fashion photography, magazine design, photojournalism and photodocumentary. His recent publications include *Fashion Spreads — word and image in fashion photography since 1980* (Berg, 1999), *Graphic Design — reproduction and representation since 1800* (Manchester University Press, 1996) and *Bodies of Experience: Gender and identity in women's photography since 1970* (Scarlet, 1997). He is also a regular contributor of articles and reviews to the *Journal of Design History* and *Fashion Theory*, and has spoken at many conferences in the UK and overseas. He is currently writing a book for Berg on advertising fashion and masculinities in Britain during the twentieth century, which will be published in spring 2004.

KATHE KOWALSKI, born Paterson, New Jersey, USA, 1945; gained her MFA in Photography from East Michigan University in 1985. She is currently a tenured Associate Professor of Photography in the Art department, Edinboro University, Pennsylvania, USA. Her work is in the collections of the Museet for Fotokunst, Denmark; the Musée de la Photographie, Charleroi, Belgium; and, in the USA, the Denver Art Museum, the Erie Art Museum, Murray State University, Edinboro University, Clarion University, Eastern Michigan University, and the Kresge Art Museum at Michigan State University. Her numerous exhibitions include solo shows in Illinois, Ohio, Iowa, Nevada,

New York, California, Missouri, Texas, Michigan and Pennsylvania. She has received numerous grants and awards for her work, and has exhibited regionally, nationally and internationally.

LAURIE LONG, born Castro Valley, California, USA, 1960; gained her BA History of Art from U.C. Berkeley in 1983, and an MFA in Photography from San Francisco State University in 1996. She lives in California and works with photography, video, sculpture, installation and performance. Her work has been widely exhibited in the USA and Europe. She has been the recipient of residencies in New York, Germany, Austria, Portugal and the Czech Republic. Humour, pop culture and feminism are key issues in her artwork. She is currently photographing goddess sites throughout Europe and fabricating fake relics.

SANDRA MATTHEWS, born New Haven, Connecticut, USA, 1951; gained her BA in Visual and Environmental Studies from Harvard University and a MFA from the State University of New York at Buffalo. She is an artist, writer, curator and Associate Professor of Film and Photography at Hampshire College in Amherst, Massachusetts. She is co-author (with Laura Wexler) of *Pregnant Pictures* (Routledge, 2000), and has published articles on photography and culture in *Afterimage* and *Exposure*. Her photocollages have been widely exhibited and she curated the exhibition *Visits to the Homeland: Photographs of China*, which travelled under the auspices of the Visual Studies Workshop Travelling Exhibition Programme.

TRISH MORRISSEY, born Dublin, Ireland, 1967; gained her MA Photography from the London College of Printing in

2001. Trish has been living and working in London since 1989. Her work has been included in many group exhibitions throughout the UK and Europe: in 1996, *Double Vie, Double Vue* at the Fondation Cartier pour l'art contemporain, Paris, curated by Patrick Rogiers; and, in 1998, *The English seen by the English* in Arles, curated by Val Williams and Gabriel Bauret. She has also been awarded numerous prizes, including UK winner of the Kodak European Young Photographer of the Year, 1994, and runner-up in the John Kobal Portrait Award in 1998. She has exhibited *WWM* at Viewpoint Gallery, Salford, in 1999, at Tom Blau Gallery, London, in 2000, and at Fotofest, Naarden, Holland in 2003.

KATE NEWTON, born Newton Abbott, Devon, England, 1967; gained her joint BA (Hons) in Photography and Design History from Staffordshire University. Since 1994 she has played a major role in the expansion and development of IRIS, and was appointed Director in 2000. She has curated touring exhibitions, coordinated internet projects and organised a national women's photographic conference. She has co-edited *I Spy — Representations of Childhood* (I. B. Tauris, 2000), *Shifting Horizons — Women's Landscape Photography Now* (I. B. Tauris, 2000) *and Ta(l)king Pictures — Thinking Through Photographs* (Questions Publishing, 2003). She also lectures in photographic theory and practice.

MAGALI NOUGAREDE, born Mantes La Jolie, France, 1969; gained her BA (Hons) in Editorial Photography from the University of Brighton in 1996. She works as a photographic artist and educator, giving lectures and talks, and also runs photography workshops in the community. She has worked extensively with adults with mental health difficulties. Her work focuses largely on exploring notions of cultural identity, transience and 'middle-classness'. Her work *Toeing the Line* stems from a Photoworks commission and was exhibited at the Towner Art Gallery, Eastbourne in January, 2001, and at Impressions Gallery in York in February, 2002. *Toeing the Line* exists as a Photoworks publication distributed by Cornerhouse. This series combines seaside landscapes with portraits of women and young girls encountered in coastal towns, and looks at the physical, psychological and geographical passage in the lives of women.

SARAH PUCILL, born Chalfont St Peter, Buckinghamshire, England, 1961; gained her MA in Fine Art from the Slade, London, in 1990. She is currently Senior Lecturer at the University of Westminster on the Fine Art BA. Since 1990 she has been making short films that have been funded by the Arts Council, and the AHRB. Her films have been televised, won awards at festivals and exhibited in galleries internationally. Venues for retrospective screenings have included the Tate Gallery and the Lux. Her photographic work, pursued between film projects, has been collected by the Saatchi Collection.

CHRISTINE ROLPH, born Glasgow, Scotland, 1959; gained her BA (Hons) History of Art and Design in 1999 from Staffordshire University. She has worked in education within the gallery sector and has experience of international conference coordination. She lectures in Contextual Studies at both Higher and Further education level. She joined IRIS as Research Associate (part-time) in March 2000, and is committed to playing a major role in its long-term development.

ZINEB SEDIRA, born Gennevilliers, France; gained her BA in Critical Fine Art Practice from Central Saint Martin's School of Art, London, in 1995 and her MA at the Slade School of Art, London, in 1997. Her research degree in Photography from the Royal College of Art was awarded in 2003. Her work explores the paradoxes and intersections of her identity as a French Algerian and as an English resident. She investigates issues of gender, representation, family, language and memory. She questions and repositions familiar Arabic-Islamic/Western images, icons and rituals within her family's 'remembered histories' and in particular the mother-daughter relationship. The veil, and the concept of the 'mental veil', is negotiated within her own experience, but extends to, the 'political' and the 'personal', the historical and the contemporary, the Eastern and the Western. She uses lens-based media to research traditional conventions of 'portraiture'. This leads her to examine issues around visibility, censorship and self-censorship through image, narrative and spoken language.

MARLA SWEENEY, born Massachusetts, USA, 1968; gained her MFA in Photography from State University of New York in 1996. Currently lives in New York and works as a photographer. She has exhibited widely in the USA and in Europe. Her work has been published in *Zoom*, *Fotomagazin* and *Camera Austria*. Her works are also in numerous collections including Musée de la Photographie, Charleroi, Belgium, Museu da Imagem, Braga, Portugal, and the Museum of Fine Arts, Houston, Texas. She is represented by Yossi Milo Gallery in New York City.

JANE TORMEY, born Watford, Herts, 1951; studied Fine Art at Wolverhampton Polytechnic and the University of Northumbria, Newcastle (MA). She is Programme Leader of Foundation Studies in Art and Design at Loughborough University. She co-edits *Tracey – Contemporary Drawing Issues*, an electronic journal, providing a focus for all aspects of drawing research. Her principal research is concerned with constructions of psychological focus in the photographic portrait and she is currently engaged with an AHRB funded project, researching the late Polaroid portraits of Walker Evans. She has published in the *International Journal of Art and Design Education (iJADE)* and submits editorials and reviews for *Tracey*.

MIRANDA WALKER, born Dorking, Surrey, 1943; studied HND Documentary Photography at Newport College of Art, 1993, and gained an MA in Documentary Photography from University of Wales College, Newport, in 1998. Exhibitions of her work include *Diverse Signals*, curated by Sue Grayson-Ford (toured 1995) and *Viewfindings*, curated by Liz Wells (toured 1994-5). Her work has been described as 'extended documentary' as she stretches realism to explore both chosen issues and the medium itself.

ACKNOWLEDGEMENTS

We would like to thank the following people and organisations:

Arts Council England and Staffordshire University for their continued support and financial contribution to this publication; Debra Klomp and Christopher Coppock for their valuable input into the selection process and commitment to the project as a whole; Catherine Fehily for her vision and input into the original concept of the *Ellipsis* series; Wendy Watriss and Fred Baldwin, FotoFest Houston for inviting us to review at the Meeting Place, which added a new dimension to the selection process.

Many thanks to the following galleries and artists whose help and generosity was invaluable in securing all the illustrative images: Kirsten Dunne, Frith Street Gallery; Elisa Kay, Lisson Gallery; Jenni Holder, Edwynn Houk Gallery; Samira Kafals, Artangel; Rhodri Morgan, Llyfyrgell Genedlaethol Cymru/National Library of Wales; Belinda Williams, Media 19; and the photographers: Rineke Dijkstra, Kay Goodridge, Alma Lopez, Rosy Martin, Delilah Montoya, Sheila Pinkel, Isabella Ramsay, Meridel Rubenstein, Karin Sander, Helen Sear and Alexa Wright.

Magali Nougarede would like to acknowledge Photoworks who commissioned her *Toeing the Line* series. Sarah Pucill would like to credit her technical assistant Helen Arthur who actually clicked the shutter.

Ffotogallery is supported by the Arts Council of Wales and Cardiff County Council.

ARTS COUNCIL
ENGLAND

Staffordshire
UNIVERSITY

CEFNOGI CREADIGRWYDD
CYNGOR CELFYDDYDAU CYMRU
THE ARTS COUNCIL OF WALES
SUPPORTING CREATIVITY